Everybody's Historic England

Everybody's Historic England

A History and Guide

Jonathan Kiek

Foreword by Michael Wood

Maps and Drawings by David Cheepen

Published in association with SUN LIFE

Q

Quiller Press
London

For Lynda, Timothy, Miranda and my parents.

Maps and drawings dedicated to the memory of Harry Cheepen

Jonathan Kiek teaches History at Watford Grammar School. He has also written *Everybody's Historic London.*
David Cheepen, who has worked as an architectural draughtsman, exhibits his drawings and paintings at Portal Gallery, Grafton Street, London W1. He teaches Art, part-time, at Watford Grammar School.

'England is a nation of shopkeepers'

Napoleon Bonaparte 1769–1821

Quoting Adam Smith, the French dictator certainly underestimated the resourceful and innovative aspects of the English. Inevitably, the rest was history.

It could be argued that Bonaparte had it half right. Except that some small businesses often grow much larger.

The Sun Life Group had small beginnings in 1810. Its empire stretched no further than two rooms facing the Bank of England in the City of London. Today the Group is one of the country's leading financial services companies with branches and customers throughout this 'green and pleasant land'. It is therefore wholly appropriate that the Group should be closely associated with Mr Kiek's exemplary 'Everybody's Historic England'.

First Published 1988
by Quiller Press Ltd
50 Albemarle Street
London W1X 4BD

Copyright © 1988 Jonathan Kiek

ISBN 0 907621 88 0

Designed in association with Book Production
Consultants, 47 Norfolk Street, Cambridge CB1 2LE

Phototypeset by Witwell Ltd, Southport

Printed by Richard Clay (The Chaucer Press) Ltd, Bungay, Suffolk

Contents

Acknowledgements

This book was an exercise in collaboration of various kinds. I wish to thank my wife for her unfailing support and encouragement — I shall cherish the memory of our journey round England in the summer of '87. I am grateful to my mother for typing most of the manuscript. I also appreciated the assistance of my father, who shows unflagging energy. David Cheepen worked tirelessly on maps and drawings. Chris Mountford drove many miles in the cause of producing fine photographs. I am indebted (for the second time) to John Fisher of the Guildhall Library, and also to Diane Courtney of the English Tourist Board. Bridget Lyne again cheerfully undertook typing, much with little time to spare. Finally, I wish to thank collaborators I do not name, and the many who in different ways have fostered my awareness of the 'Historic England' surrounding us.

Jonathan Kiek

Foreword

Local history is the stuff of life as far as the writing of history is concerned. Every one of our rural or urban communities has reacted and contributed in its own way to the mainstream of British history. So, as each new generation grows up, it is essential that they are encouraged to look afresh at the living history around them. The best way to start is to be inspired by books and then to travel about and see for yourself: at least that is how it happened for me, and I'm sure it is true of most people. Jonathan Kiek has already enthused us with his thorough, readable and *usable* book on London, which turned up many nooks and crannies of the capital's history which must have escaped even the diehard searcher after its history. Now he has turned his attention to the country as a whole, providing a guide for the prospective traveller into the British past. It is a laudable enterprise – for the past must always be reinterpreted – and I hope it will meet the same success as his previous work.

Michael Wood

Michael Wood

Introduction

This is a companion to *Everybody's Historic London*, and it essentially follows the same scheme. Swiftly surveyed periods precede 'Historic England' sections, which mainly comprise guide material. Fifteen tours are suggested at the end.

Some readers may be encouraged to explore our past more deeply. The broad sweep of English history has sometimes been encompassed in single volumes. J.R. Green's *Short History of the English People* was first published over a hundred years ago. G.M. Trevelyan's *History of England* (Longman, 3rd edition 1945) will always be read, and, for 'history of a people with the politics missed out', so will his *Illustrated English Social History* (Penguin 1949–52). In recent times, historians have tended to eschew the broad sweep – so widening the gap between 'academic' and 'popular' history. *The English Experience* by John Bowle (Weidenfeld and Nicolson, 1971) and *A Social History of England* by Asa Briggs (Weidenfeld and Nicolson, 1983) are two exceptions.

The history of England is more usually covered by series of volumes. Of these the Oxford History is the most established and – literally! – weighty. The Pelican History (Penguin) is worth its (smaller) weight in gold. Excellent collective histories are produced by Longman, Nelson and Arnold.

To this general category belong the Methuen series on English Monarchs, and the older, far less detailed, Fontana volumes, which began with Christopher Brooke's *Saxon and Norman Kings* and ended with *Hanover to Windsor* by Roger Fulford.

For history county by county, the massive Victoria History of the Counties of England nestles in your local library. The county books of Arthur Mee's *The King's England* (Hodder) have recently been revised.

In *The Making of the English Landscape* (Hodder, 1955; Penguin, 1970), W.G. Hoskins described what could be called 'the history of England's geography'. Many have followed on, including Richard Muir in *The Shell Guide to Reading the Landscape* (Michael Joseph,

1981). Muir had previously written about *The English Village* (Thames and Hudson, 1980). The development of towns is surveyed by David W. Lloyd in *The Making of English Towns* (Gollancz/Peter Crawley, 1984). Towns of special architectural interest were explored by Alex Clifton-Taylor in memorable books (B.B.C. Publications, 1978, 1981 and 1984). For architecture there is Pevsner's classic series *The Buildings of England* (Penguin). *The English House* by James Chambers (Thames Methuen, 1985) is a well illustrated survey of the main developments.

Guide books abound – a growth industry of our time! At the market's glossy end, AA and Shell lead the way. The Ordnance Survey Leisure Guides (AA) are a good example. Less glossy, and most informative, are the Blue Guides, including the Blue Guide to England. For some on their journeys, the Egon Ronay Pub Guide will be indispensable!

Informal, discursive guides include H.V. Morton's *In Search of England* (Methuen, 1927), the first (recently reissued) of his famous series. *Everybody's Historic England* is, like its companion, a 'discriminating beginner's course'. In this case the field work comprises fifteen suggested tours to different parts of the country. At Dover the Roman Painted House displays the admonition that 'A country which destroys its past deserves to have no future'. In fact, there is no danger of this – whether we like it or not, the past (and not merely in a material sense) will always permeate our present. It is essential for everybody, both by reading and by travelling, to find out more about it.

1 Landmarks in the History of England

43	Start of Roman occupation
60	Boudicca's Revolt
209	Alban, England's first Christian martyr, executed
312	Christianity made legal in Roman Empire
383	Hadrian's Wall abandoned
410	Roman troops withdrawn
597	Arrival of Augustine
633	Birth of Cuthbert
635	Aidan settles on Lindisfarne
664	Council of Whitby
685	Cuthbert made Bishop of Lindisfarne
c698	The Lindisfarne Gospels
735	Death of Bede
793	Danes raid Holy Island
796	Death of Offa
849	Birth of Alfred
867	Danes capture York (start of Jorvik)
871	Battle of Ashdown
878	Battle of Edington (Ethandun)
937	Battle of Brunanburh
943	Dunstan made Abbot of Glastonbury
954	Battle of Stainmore
978	Edward the Martyr assassinated
1016	Cnut succeeds Ethelred the Unready
1066	Battle of Hastings
1079	Winchester Cathedral begun
1086	Domesday Survey
1093	Durham Cathedral begun
1135	Start of Cistercian community at Fountains
(-54)	Civil War
1154	Henry II (-89)
1170	Murder of Becket
1174	Fire at Canterbury Cathedral

1185	Earthquake shakes Lincoln
1215	Magna Carta
1220	Salisbury Cathedral begun (consecrated 1258)
1263	Balliol College, Oxford founded
1264	Simon de Montfort defeats Henry III at Battle of Lewes
1265	Battle of Evesham
1327	Edward II murdered at Berkeley Castle
	Edward III (-77)
1348	Edward founds Order of the Garter
(-51)	The Black Death
1381	The Peasants' Revolt
1382	Wyclif condemned (dies 1384)
1399	Richard II murdered at Pontefract Castle
1403	Battle of Shrewsbury
1415	Battle of Agincourt
1446	King's College Chapel begun
1450	End of the Hundred Years War
1455	1st Battle of St. Albans
1460	Battle of Wakefield
1461	2nd Battle of St. Albans
	Battle of Towton
1470(-71)	Readeption of Henry VI
1471	Battles of Barnet and Tewkesbury
1485	Battle of Bosworth
1487	Battle of Stoke
1497	Perkin Warbeck captured
1509	Henry VIII (-47)
1518	Death of Thomas Paycocke
1525	Tyndale's English New Testament
1529	Fall of Wolsey
1536	Lesser monasteries dissolved
	Catharine of Aragon dies
	Pilgrimage of Grace
1539	Greater monasteries suppressed
1549	Western Rebellion (against Cranmer's Book of Common Prayer)
	Ket's (Anti-Enclosure) Rebellion
1556	Burning of Cranmer
1558	Elizabeth 1 (-1603)
1559	Religious Settlement
1564	Birth of Shakespeare
1567	Longleat begun
1569	Revolt of the Northern Earls

1575	Leicester entertains Elizabeth at Kenilworth
1579	Saxton's Map of England and Wales
1582	Shakespeare leaves Stratford for London
1586	Publication of Camden's *Britannia*
1587	Execution of Mary Queen of Scots
1588	Defeat of Spanish Armada
1597	Bess (Elizabeth, Countess of Shrewsbury) moves into Hardwick Hall
1602	Bodleian Library founded
1605	Gunpowder Plot. Arrest of conspirators at Holbeche House (Staffs)
1607	Hatfield House begun
1611	Shakespeare retires to Stratford
1628	Petition of Right
1640	Long Parliament meets
1642	Outbreak of Civil War (-46)
	Battle of Edgehill
1643	Battle of Chalgrove Field
	1st Battle of Newbury
1644	Battle of Marston Moor
1645	Battle of Naseby
1647	The Putney Debates
1649	Execution of Charles I
	Suppression of Levellers at Burford
1649(-60)	The Interregnum
1652	George Fox climbs Pendle Hill
1660	The Restoration
1665	The Great Plague
1685	Battle of Sedgemoor – last battle on English soil
1688–9	The Glorious Bloodless Revolution
1700	Richard Gough starts *The History of Myddle*
	Castle Howard begun (completed 1737)
1705	Beau Nash arrives in Bath
1709	Abraham Darby perfects smelting of iron with coke
1714	The Hanoverian Succession (George 1–1727)
1718(-22)	Silk mill built at Derby for John and Thomas Lombe
1721(-42)	Walpole P.M.
1739	Start (at Bristol) of John Wesley's Open Air Mission
1745	(2nd) Jacobite Rebellion — Bonnie Prince Charlie turns back at Derby
1760	George III (—1820)
1761	James Brindley constructs the Bridgwater Canal (later ex-

	tended to Mersey estuary at Runcorn). Start of Canal network
1764	James Hargreaves invents the Spinning Jenny.
	'Capability' Brown landscapes grounds at Blenheim Palace
1765	Matthew Boulton opens factory at Soho (outside Birmingham)
1768	Richard Arkwright builds spinning mill at Nottingham
1769	Josiah Wedgwood opens factory at Etruria
1771	Birth of Robert Owen (d.1858)
	Opening of Arkwright's Mill at Cromford (Derbys)
1776	Birth of John Constable (d.1837)
	'Coke of Norfolk' starts to farm Holkham estate
1779	World's 1st iron bridge cast at Coalbrookdale
1783	1st visit of the Prince of Wales to Brighton
1791	Tom Paine's *The Rights of Man* (Part 1)
1799	Wordsworth returns to the Lakes
1805	Battle of Trafalgar
1811–13	Luddite Riots
1815	Battle of Waterloo
1819	The 'Peterloo' Massacre
1822	William Cobbett begins his Rural Rides
1830	Opening of Manchester and Liverpool Railway
1832	Great Reform Bill
1834	Trial of Tolpuddle Martyrs
1835	I.K. Brunel appointed Chief Engineer to the G.W.R. (Completed 1841)
1836	Start of Chartism
1837	Victoria (-1901)
1848	End of Chartism
	The Communist Manifesto
1859	*The Origin of Species, Self Help, Essay on Liberty*
1867	2nd Reform Act
1870	Start of State elementary education
1872	Introduction of Secret Ballot
1878	Joseph Swan invents electric lighting
1879	1st Telephone Exchange
1896	1st property acquired by the National Trust (The Clergy House, Afriston)
	Red Flag Act repealed
1897	Diamond Jubilee
1899	Outbreak of (2nd) Boer War (-1902)
	Rowntree's 1st Survey of York

1909	Lloyd George's 'People's Budget'
1914	Outbreak of World War One
1916	Battle of The Somme
1918	The Armistice
	Women over 30 receive vote
1922	B.B.C. established
1926	The General Strike
1927	First 'talkie' pictures
1928	Discovery of penicillin
1929	The Wall Street Crash
1933	J.B. Priestley's *English Journey*
1936	The Jarrow March
	The General Theory of Employment, Interest and Money
1939	Discovery of Sutton Hoo Ship Burial
	Outbreak of World War Two
1940	Churchill P.M. (-45)
	Battle of Britain
	Coventry bombed
1942	The Beveridge Report
1944	Butler's Education Act
1945	End of War. Attlee P.M. (-51)
1948	National Health Service
1952	Elizabeth II
1956	Coventry Cathedral begun (completed 1962)
1959	M1 opened, England's 1st motorway
1964	Wilson P.M. (–70. Again 74–76)
1965	Death of Churchill
1967	Milton Keynes inaugurated
1977	Silver Jubilee
1979	Thatcher P.M.
1982	The Falklands War
1984	Fire at York Minster
1985	The Handsworth Riots
1987	Start of 3rd Thatcher term

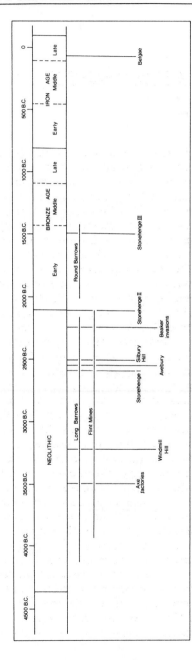

Time Chart 4500 BC – 0 (David Cheepen)

2 From Stone to Iron

The New Stone Age settlers, who arrived here around 4000 BC, left some seemingly indelible footprints on the sands of time. In Wiltshire one can see a concentration of powerful reminders. Stonehenge on Salisbury Plain and the stone circle at Avebury originated in the New Stone Age. Close to Avebury is the causewayed enclosure, three bank-and-ditch rings with linking causeways, on Windmill Hill, which is probably even older (c 3250 BC) than Avebury itself. This could have been a meeting place and a centre for trade. The nearby long barrow at West Kennet, a collective tomb made of Sarsen stones, belongs to the same period – it is therefore older than the Egyptian pyramids. Neighbouring Silbury Hill, the largest artificial mound in Europe, would have taken 18 million hours of labour to build. We don't known what it was for – prehistory is shrouded in mystery (which helps to explain its fascination). Like Avebury and Stonehenge, many of the fortified hill forts, notably Maiden Castle in Dorset, originated in the New Stone Age.

The Roman historian, Tacitus, wrote dismissively: 'Who the first inhabitants of Britain were, whether natives or immigrants, remain obscure. One must remember that we are dealing with barbarians.' In fact a partial picture is possible of the people who began the henges and hillforts. They came to live in upland areas, like the Chilterns and Cotswolds, where there were fewer trees to clear. Their way of life was more settled than that of the hunters of the Old Stone Age. This change from the nomadic, hunting existence to one of keeping animals and sowing primitive wheat and barley is known as the Neolithic Revolution, though the Neolithic farmers would have hunted as well as farmed. They made pottery, and they mined flints. At Grime's Graves in Norfolk the pits, excavated by antler picks, are fifty feet deep. The flints were traded along with livestock, hides and polished axe-heads. There were centres of axe-head production, the axe-factories, from where axe-heads, important for land clearance, were sent all over the country. This wasn't their only use in Neolithic times. At Maiden Castle, Sir Mortimer Wheeler found a youth's skeleton – 'the bones bore many axe marks and the whole body had

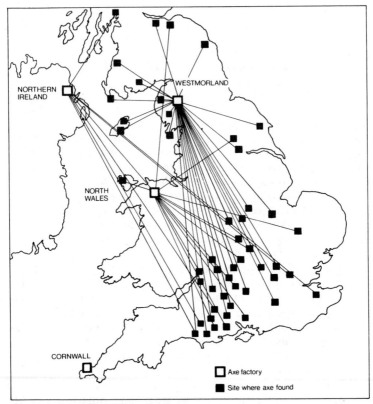

Axe Factories (David Cheepen)

been cut up as by a butcher for the stew-pot...' The farmers of the New Stone Age were capable of cannibalism.

The making of bronze (an alloy of copper and tin) was common in England by about 1700 BC, roughly two thousand years after its introduction in the Near East. The origin of this development is linked with the Beaker People (named after the drinking mugs found in their graves) who around 2500 BC arrived here with bronze weapons. Archaeology has built up the impression that War was no stranger to the Bronze Age Society they ushered in – the bronze was worth fighting for. This state of strife would have encouraged the emergence of leaders, and the existence of a 'chieftain society' may be inferred from the plentiful round barrows. In contrast to the Neolithic long barrows, these were graves of individuals, important people who, like Egyptian pharaohs, were buried with valuables.

Many round barrows may be seen in the area around Stonehenge. This impressive structure, the greatest monument of European prehistory, was developed from simple Neolithic beginnings by the stupendous labours of the Bronze Age, the transformation being initiated by the Beaker People. So gigantic an undertaking points to the organizing role of the wealthy and powerful individuals who ended up in the round barrows. This wealth, which gave them their power, came from the trade in bronze. Bronze was traded to Europe – and beyond – in return for the previous goods that might also end up in the round barrows. Like Stonehenge, the stone circle at Avebury was developed in the Bronze Age, though far less dramatically.

With the use of iron, the trade in bronze at last declined. The aristocracy of the Bronze Age fell on permanent hard times, being eclipsed, about two thousand years after the influx of Beaker People, by waves of immigrants using iron weapons and implements. These were the Celts, who started to arrive about 650 BC.

Our image of the Celts has been influenced by their enemies, and eventual masters, the Romans, who naturally gave them a poor press. The English imperial view of African or Indian subjects in the 19th century would have been equally one-sided. 'All the Britons,' wrote Julius Ceasar, 'dye their bodies with woad, which produces a blue colour, and this gave them a more terrifying appearance in battle.'

Skilled in chariot warfare, they were undoubtedly terrifying to the Roman legions. Celtic hill-forts of chalk, stone and timber, like Maiden Castle (there were many others, such as Hambledon Hill, Hod Hill and Eggardun [Dorset], Bredon [Shropshire] and Barbury Camp [Wilts]) would have seemed formidable obstacles.

But the Celts should be seen in a more than military light. In peacetime, the hill forts were simply hilltop villages. They also lived in settled villages away from hilltops. An example is Chysauster in the far west of Cornwall, an excavated Celtic village (from the second century BC) consisting of houses of granite dry-walling still several feet high.*[1] It was the Celts who introduced the primitive plough, which made the small, roughly rectangular fields that still survive in some parts, notably in the Sussex Downs, where there are $11\frac{1}{2}$ square miles just north of Brighton. In the far west of Cornwall one can still see the rubble walling bounding the fields of surviving Celtic farmsteads.

The Celts were adept at pottery, weaving and metalwork. They learned to produce pottery on a fast-turning wheel, while weaving was carried out on upright looms with clay weights and bone combs.

---

*[1]Chyauster Ancient Village ($2\frac{1}{2}$ m NW of Gulval off B3311) is an English Heritage property.

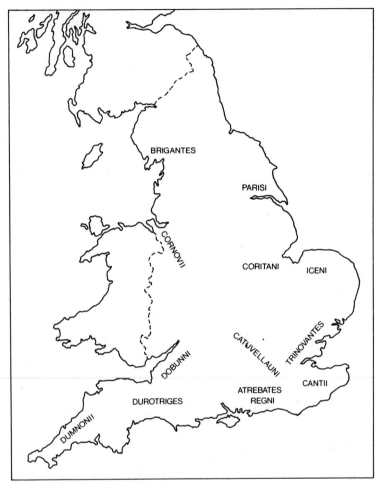

Celtic tribes at the time of Claudius' invasion (David Cheepen)

The Desborough Mirror, from Northants, which may be seen at the British Museum, exemplifies the fine work of Celtic metal-smiths.

The Iron Age Celts didn't bequeath magnificent ruins – their greatest hill-forts may convey a sense of mystery, but are hardly imposing to the modern visitor.*² They did leave behind the magnificent white horse, cut above Uffington on the Berkshire Downs, close to the prehistoric Ridgeway route. It's clearly a racehorse – doubtless

---

*² See *A Guide to the Hill-forts of Britain* A.H.A. Hogg (Paladin)

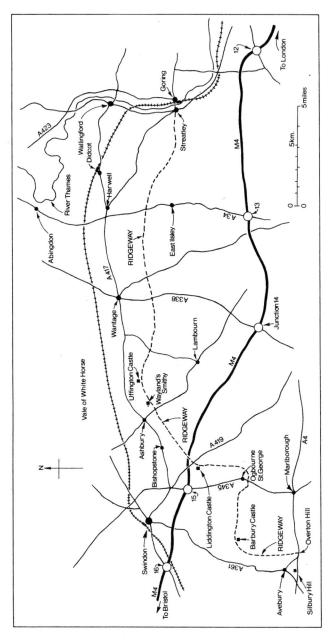

The Ridgeway (David Cheepen)

modelled on the Red Rum of the day! The Celts are supposed to have loved racehorses, even believing that horse racing would be enjoyed in the afterlife.

Further Reading

Iron Age Communities in Britain Barry Cunliffe (Routledge, 1974)
Celtic Britain Lloyd Laing (Routledge, 1979)
Prehistoric Stone Circles Aubrey Burl (Shire Archaeology, 1979)
The Oldest Road, An Exploration of The Ridgeway J.R.L. Anderson and Fay Godwin (Wildwood House, London, 1975)

3 Historic England (1)

Avebury

The stone circle at Avebury was a prehistoric henge (a circular area, for a ritual purpose, surrounded by a bank and ditch). The fact that the fosse (ditch) is on the inside of the high circular earthwork (bank) suggests that this largely Neolithic structure, which the Beaker People may have completed, had a religious, rather than a military, purpose.

On the inside of the ditch stands what is left of a huge circle of un-shaped megaliths (Greek *mega* – large; *Lithos* – stone). The Sarsen stones, like those at Stonehenge, probably came from **Fyfield Down** and **Overton Down** two or three miles to the east. The term 'Sarsen' derives from 'Saracen'. In Crusade stories the Saracens (Turks) were regarded as magicians, and to medieval eyes the Sarsen stones had appeared as if by magic. From this circle, which surrounds the village of Avebury, an avenue of stones leads beyond the **West Kennet Long Barrow** to **the Sanctuary**, a circular site on **Overton Hill**.

Stonehenge

The early (Neolithic) Stonehenge (c 3000 BC) was essentially a circular space (much smaller than at Avebury) enclosed by a bank and ditch, with an entrance on the north-east side. On the inside edge of the ditch were the **Aubrey Holes**, a ring of 56 pits, named after the 17th-century antiquarian who discovered them.

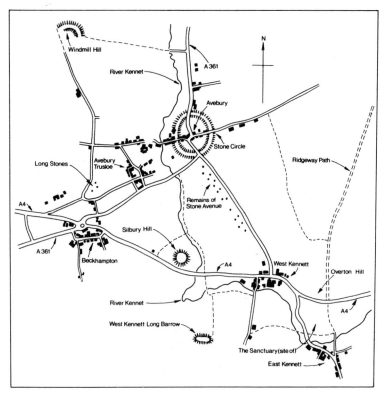

Avebury and surrounding area (David Cheepen)

Around 2500 BC, in the twilight of the Stone Age, the bronze-bearing Beaker People built the Avenue linking Stonehenge with the Avon. They brought bluestones from the Prescelley Mountains in Wales, via the Bristol Channel and River Avon, a distance, as the crow flies, of 140 miles. These they began to erect in a double circle, but for some reason the task wasn't completed. The holes where bluestones once stood lie on either side of the bluestone circle we see today.

The great Sarsen stones, dragged on rollers from the Marlborough Downs, arrived a long time after the bluestones. The horseshoe of trilithons (doorways) would have been raised before the Sarsen circle. Later the bluestones were arranged in the circle and horse-shoe whose remains we see today. This was after digging holes (the Y

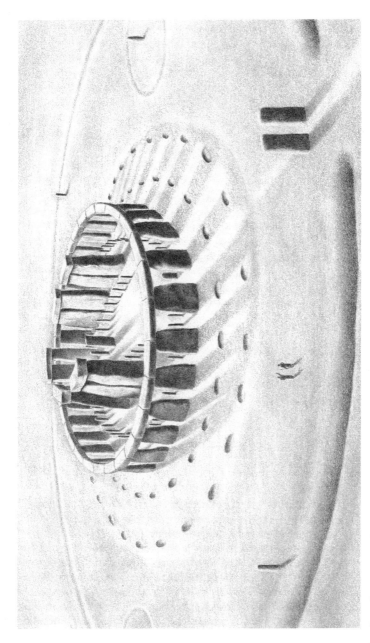

Stonehenge – reconstructed (David Cheepen)

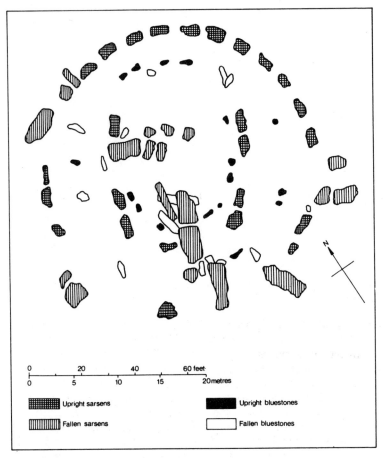

Stonehenge – as it is (David Cheepen)

and Z holes) in two rings outside the Sarsen circle. These were designed to take bluestones – it seems that Bronze Age architects were perfectly capable of changing their minds! The Sarsens and the bluestones in the horseshoe were shaped and smoothed – contrast Avebury. The Sarsens were joined together by fitting the knobs (tenons) on top of the uprights into the corresponding holes (mortises) in the under sides of the lintels.

The key question – what Stonehenge was for – is unanswerable. If we assume it was some kind of temple – a Bronze Age York Minster

D. Cheepen 1. 11. 1986.

Avebury, Wiltshire – 'as much surpassing Stonehenge,' wrote John Aubrey, 'as a cathedral doth a parish church.'

– what kind of worship went on? The fact that the heel stone, the large boulder in its natural state outside the bank, is orientated on the midsummer sunrise suggests a possible connection with sun-worship. It's likely that Stonehenge was also a political centre, where Bronze Age chiefs presided over their courts. Recently it has been suggested that Stonehenge was a large analogue computer for a prediction of eclipses. Such an interpretation may tell us more about contemporary preoccupations. 'It stands,' wrote Henry James, 'as lonely in history as it does on the great plain.' The whole truth will remain elusive – we're left to ponder the mystery.

Maiden Castle

The biggest of the Celtic hill forts, Maiden Castle, near Weymouth in Dorset, was originally a Neolithic causewayed camp, similar to Windmill Hill. From 500 BC it was heavily fortified by Iron Age warriors. Maze-like entrances at the east and west ends were designed to thwart attackers, but in AD 43 Maiden Castle was successfully stormed by the Romans. This wasn't the end of the settlement, for a Roman temple of the 4th century has been excavated near the top of the hill.

27

4 The Romans

In 55 BC Roman legions forced a landing on the shingly shore near Dover. On this occasion they didn't linger because rebellion was simmering in Gaul. Caesar was back again the following year, when resistance was spearheaded by the Catuvellauni, led by Cassivellaunus, one of the Belgic group of Celtic tribes, who had only recently arrived in England. The Belgae did not generally build hill-forts, instead enclosing areas of land behind dykes. Cassivellaunus' main stronghold, possibly at Wheathampstead (Herts), was captured by Caesar, who then returned to Gaul.

In AD 43 the Romans landed at Richborough, then advanced on Colchester, the recently made capital of the Catuvellauni. After its capture the Romans built a grandiose temple whose vaults may be seen today beneath the castle the Normans would erect many centuries later. A model of this temple to Claudius is in the castle Museum.

When the Romans struck west into Dorset and Wiltshire their targets were the hill-forts, such as Cadbury Rings, Hod Hill and Maiden Castle. Even the maze-like defences of Maiden Castle proved of little use against the phalanxed legionaries. The site of Exeter (Isca Dumnoniorum) was secured as a southern base on the western frontier.

The imposition of Roman rule wasn't plain sailing – and despite what Tacitus describes as the seduction of the Celtic aristocracy by 'the lounge, the bath and the well-appointed dinner table'! In AD 60 there was perhaps a puritanical edge to Boudiccan invective against the Romans who 'sleep on soft couches with boys as bedfellows and boys past their prime at that'. Colchester (Camulodunum), St. Albans (Verulamium) and Londinium, all unfortified at this time, were destroyed by Boudicca's revolting Iceni, before they were crushed somewhere in the Midlands, close to Watling Street.

With Boudicca out of the way, Pax Romana lasted about 300 years. It was ultimately founded, not on legionary might, but upon the recognition by the native (Romano-British) aristocracy that 'they'd never had it so good', a perception influenced by the sophisti-

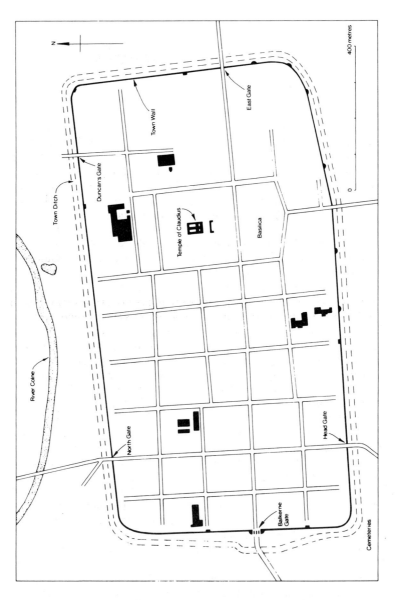

Plan of Roman Colchester – the first capital of the province (David Cheepen)

cated enjoyments of Roman town life. The Romans re-developed some towns (eg. Colchester, the earliest administrative centre of the province) and founded others. Many were garrison centres like Luguvalium (Carlisle) and Deva (Chester), or coloniae like Eboracum (York), towns built initially for retired soldiers, which grew into administrative centres. Verulamium was a municipium, or chartered city, while many, like Corinium (Cirencester), a centre of administration in the West country, belonged to none of these categories. All towns shared the Roman street plan of straight lines and right angles. The most important building was the town hall, or basilica, fronting one side of the forum, the central meeting place. Town dwellers worshipped at the temple, were entertained at the amphitheatre (at Verulamium, uniquely, the theatre) and relaxed at the baths.

Most people continued to live in small farmsteads and villages, the majority being scattered hamlets, untouched by the Roman lifestyle. However, this was carried on in scores of villas, country houses set in their own large acreage of fields. Some villas were little more than farmhouses. Others, such as Fishbourne, near Chichester (Sussex) and Lullingstone (Kent) were like palaces, with tessellated pavements and colonnades.

Ancient trackways, continuing to link many villages, were supplemented by a vast road system. Watling Street (the A5) went north-west from the Kent coast to Chester. Ermine Street (the Great North road or A1) ran from London to Corbridge near Hadrian's Wall. Fosse Way connected Lincoln to Exeter. Such roads, whose purpose was partly military – hence their straightness – could be seen as the Roman motorways. Far more were built to cater for local needs. Many of the lines of Roman roads survive, though generally not the roads themselves. Blackstone Edge, in Lancashire, is one which has.

The villa building Romano-British élite did well out of the (occupation stimulated) exploitation of native resources, such as tin in Cornwall and sheep in the Cotswolds. In some areas, like the Cotswolds, villas were the organising centres of local industrial and agricultural development. Estates were enhanced in different ways by the Roman introduction to England of, for example, roses and vines, box and laurel, and cabbages and broad beans.

Pax Romana, essential for flourishing economic activity, was increasingly fragile due to Roman divisions and barbarian attacks. Ambitious generals tried to become Emperors. Early on in this phase, it was a case at York of the young Constantine having greatness thrust upon him when his troops proclaimed him western Emperor. For a long while, and in spite of political unrest, the economy continued to

Roman roads and major towns (David Cheepen)

prosper – the Emperor Julian even enlarged the Rhineland granaries to accommodate British grain. Ominously, however, Picts, Irish and Germans co-ordinated a major attack in 367. In 383 the Romans abandoned Hadrian's Wall. The Roman forts of the Saxon Shore – Richborough, Portchester, overlooking Portsmouth Harbour, and Burgh Castle, close to the Norfolk and Suffolk border, are examples – belong to this phase. This defensive measure was in vain once the Emperor Honorius ordered the withdrawal of Roman troops to defend Rome (410). The Anglo-Saxon takeover, previously a gradual infiltration, became an irresistible flood.

Further Reading

Britannia S.S. Frere (Routledge, 1967)

Roman Britain I.A. Richmond (Penguin, 1955)

The Archaeology of Roman Britain I.A. Richmond (Methuen, 2nd edition 1969)

Roman England John Burke (The English Tourist Board/Weidenfeld and Nicolson, 1983)

Towns in Roman Britain Julian Bennett (Shire Archaeology, 1984)

Roman Roads Richard W. Bagshawe (Shire Archeology, 1979)

Hadrian's Wall (Ordnance Survey 1964)

The Roman Baths and Museum Official Guidebook

5 Historic England (2)

The Romans at Dover

Though it was at Richborough that the Romans landed in AD 43, it seems likely that Dover took over at the British end of the most direct cross-channel route from Boulogne. This is suggested by the impressive lighthouse, the earliest in England, which may be seen within the walls of Dover Castle. A headquarters fort was built at Dover for the Roman fleet.

The **Roman Painted House**, containing over 400 square feet of richly coloured wall-paintings, may well have belonged to a Roman port official or naval commander.

Verulamium (St. Albans) – A Municipium

Verulamium has a pre-Roman history. The Romans built their city close to the Belgic stronghold (in Prae Wood). This had replaced the earlier one Wheeler identified at Wheathampstead, destroyed by Caesar in 54 BC. Following the Boudiccan destruction of the first Roman Verulamium, a rampart and ditch were constructed, and later two miles of stone wall and bastions, with four gateways each with a guard-house.

33

The Abbey Church is built on the supposed site of England's first martyrdom in 209 – of St. Alban, a citizen of Verulamium who died for sheltering a Christian priest. Down by the artificial lake, there's a good view of part of the north–east section of the wall. Within a brick shelter are the remains of a bath suite with a mosaic pavement and **hypocaust** (under floor central heating). The Roman **theatre** may originally have been built for ceremonies connected with the adjacent temple, no part of which survives. Note the horseshoe shape of the arena, with a stage at the end (hence a theatre, not an amphitheatre). The smallness of the stage suggests that performances mainly took place in the arena, to which access was provided by the three gangways piercing the seating bank. These would have been vaulted over to carry seats.

Don't miss the **museum**, whose Roman treasures include mosaics and a priceless bronze statuette of Venus, as well as a large-scale model of post-Boudiccan Verulamium.

Spot the corner of the vanished **basilica** marked out close to the Museum.

Part of the North-East Wall of Roman Verulamium (Chris Mountford)

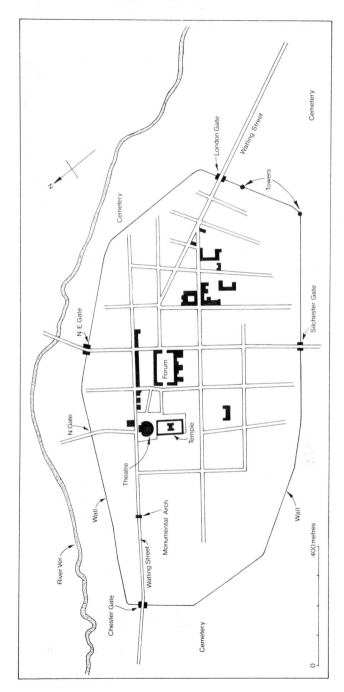

Plan of Roman Verulamium (David Cheepen)

The foundations of London Gate, Roman Verulamium. This was where Watling Street entered the city. Verulamium was a day's journey along Watling Street from London (Chris Mountford)

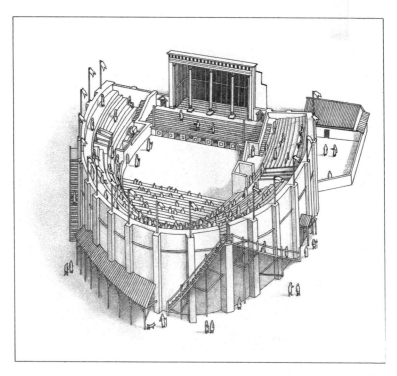

Verulamium Theatre – reconstructed (David Cheepen) (based on a drawing by Alan Sorrell)

Verulamium Theatre – as it is (Chris Mountford)

A Sample of Roman Towns

Little survives above ground of Roman Cirencester (Corinium). The museum in **Black Jack Street** contains reminders of the vanished glories, including two tombstones of cavalrymen. The inscription on Genialis's reads:

> SEXTUS VALERIUS GENIALIS, TROOPER OF THE CAVALRY REGIMENT OF THRACIANS, A FRISIAN TRIBESMAN, FROM THE TROOP OF GENIALIS, AGED 40, OF 20 YEARS SERVICE, LIES BURIED HERE. HIS HEIR HAD THIS SET UP.

(Highlighting the fact that the vast majority of the occupying army was not strictly Roman at all, but were recruited from all corners of the vast empire.)

The (now) grassy banked amphitheatre lies to the south-west of the town. Two gangways lead into the arena.

For centuries Silchester (Gloucs) was the lost Roman city. One mile to the east of present day Silchester, within a circuit of wall (with a small amphitheatre to the east) a layout of streets, with baths, temples, forum, basilica and even a Christian Church – perhaps the earliest – has been marvellously preserved.

Chester (Deva) was the base of the 20th legion. **Grosvenor Museum** has appropriately a Roman military exhibition. The City walls, like the medieval Rows, rest on Roman foundations.

Stretches of the Roman wall survive at Lincoln (Lindum), a colonia, on which many roads converged. From the **Newport Gate**, once the northern entrance to the town, traffic passed along Ermine Street to the Humber.

York (Eboracum), colonia and legionary base, was a centre of operations against Brigantes and Picts. At the close of the 2nd century, Septimius Severus made it the capital of Britannia Inferior.

York Minster stands on the site of the Roman fort, a surviving pillar of which faces the Minster's south door. **Stonegate** and **Petergate** were the two main streets of Eboracum, intersecting at the centre of the fort and leading to gates in the walls. Large remnants of those walls survive beneath the medieval layer, for example between the **Multangular Tower** and **St. Leonard's Hospital.**

Newport Arch, Lincoln (Chris Mountford)

Wall and the Multangular Tower, York. The lower part of the Tower and adjoining wall is Roman. (Chris Mountford)

Chedworth – A Fine Roman Villa

One of a number of extensive villas supported by the wealthy, wool-producing countryside surrounding prosperous Corinium, many of the original walls still stand several feet high, The principal living rooms were arranged round three sides of an inner court. The outer court may have been used as a farmyard.

From a nearby spring Chedworth derived its own water supply. Find the Chi-Rho monogram carved on the stone surround of the reservoir, from where the fresh water was taken. These Christian occupants of Chedworth were in a minority in Roman England, though Christianity was a legal religion of the Empire from 313.

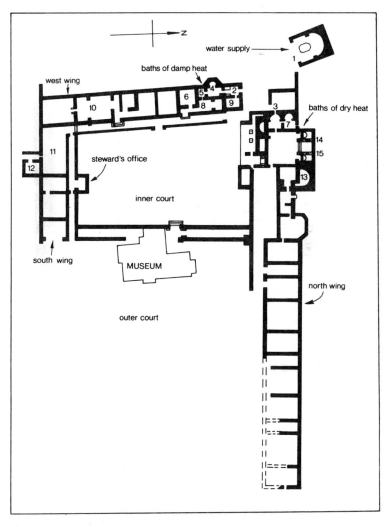

1. Nymphaeum
2. Furnace
3. Furnace
4. Caldarium
5. Tepidarium

6. Apodyterium
7. Laconicum
8. Frigidarium
9. Cold bath
10. Triclinium

11. Kitchen
12. Lavatory
13. Reception room
14. Immersion bath
15. Plunge bath

Plan of the Roman villa at Chedworth, Gloucs. (David Cheepen)

41

The Roman Baths at Bath

The temple – one of the finest in Roman England – together with the magnificent baths, were the focal points of the town of Aquae Sulis, built by the Romans on the site of a natural hot spring. The temple lies buried, but the baths can – and must! – be visited. These were not the simple baths, offering the standard facilities, but an ever-expanding complex – Hadrian's decree forbidding mixed bathing most likely necessitated the suite of rooms to the east. The centrepiece was the **great bath**, a huge swimming pool filled with warm water, around which, in the recesses (exedrae), patrons sat to exchange gossip and ideas. The reservoir containing the steaming water (c 48 c) from the spring, was sited a little below the (medieval) **king's bath**. This could be viewed from the large open hall comprising the frigidarium. (Spot the two openings in the dividing wall.)

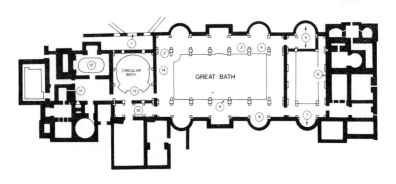

1. Roman windows
2. The culvert by which hot mineral water entered the bath
3. The Great Bath
4. The drain (to empty the Great Bath)
5. Semicircular bath
6. The Eastern baths
7. Semicircular bath
8. Alcoves (for spectators)
9. Drip gully
10. Corridor
11. Hypocaust
12. Oval swimming bath
13. Circular Bath (a cold plunge bath)
14. Vault (part of)

Plan of the Roman Baths at Bath (David Cheepen)

Hadrian's Wall

Once running a continuous 75 miles from Wallsend on Tyne in the east to Bowness on the Solway Firth in the west, a forbidding 20 feet high, and regularly punctuated with forts, milecastles and turrets, what is left of Hadrian's Wall is the strongest possible reminder of the Roman occupation. Building began in 122, and went on for about ten years. A protective ditch was dug on each side, the southern one (the **vallum**) marking the administrative boundary of the province. It also protected the soldiers' backs from the Brigantiaons – who, rather than the Picts, were the principal threat. A supply road (the **Stanegate**) ran between this ditch and the Wall.

The most intact fort is **Housesteads**, with gateways, granaries, barrack blocks and latrines – a model is in the Housesteads **Museum**. Walk the well-trodden westward stretch from here to the meeting of the Pennine Way and the Wall. This takes in **Milecastle** 37 and the marvellous view from **Cuddy's Crag**.

Vindolanda (Chesterholm)*, one of the Stanegate fortifications, is situated a couple of miles south of the Wall. A reconstruction of a

The North Granary, Housesteads. The short upright pillars were part of the ventilation system. They are not to be confused with a hypocaust. (Chris Mountford)

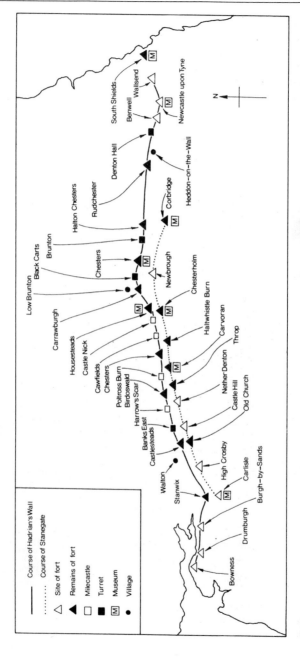

Plan of Hadrian's Wall (David Cheepen)

turret and a section of the wall has been set up on the south side. Outside the fort are excavated remains of a large civilian settlement (the *Vicus*). The **museum** is excellent.

If you have the opportunity, drive the full length of the Wall – the immense achievement of the Romans will become more forcibly apparent.

*See *An Illustrated Guide* by Robin Birley.

Vindolanda. To the south of the site are replicas of Hadrian's Wall. The size of the stone turret shows how large and formidable the Wall once was. (Chris Mountford)

6 Medieval England

The Anglo-Saxon Chronicle records that 'the Britons fled from the English like fire'. As the Arthurian legends suggest, there was rearguard action – rather like Hereward the Wake's after the Norman Conquest – but it proved fruitless. The Britons were driven west. One Saxon colonist, with the British name of Cerdic, landed at Southampton Water and worked his way to Wiltshire, going on to found the Cerdinga monarchy of Wessex, which united England, and from which our royal line descends. The settlement poses many questions, but the 'Dark Ages' – the name given to this period, about which we chiefly speculate – wasn't all doom and destruction. We do know, for example, that buildings were being restored in Verulamium in the 5th century. Fairly rapid recovery is suggested by the evidence of the 7th-century Sutton Hoo Ship burial. This marvellous treasure (displayed in the British Museum) probably belonged to the mighty Raedwald, King of the East Angles (died c.624).

The chief association of Roman England is with sophisticated town life. In fact most of England was woodland, and the main achievement of the early Anglo-Saxons was to clear a great part of it, sometimes by burning, but more usually with their axes. Almost every English village today existed by 1066, largely owing to determined Saxon toil. The Domesday Book of 1086 (to be seen at the Public Record office in London) lists about 13,000. Many have disappeared since then, and many have changed hugely, though not totally out of recognition. The village green was probably in origin a defensive enclosure. (Such greens are to be found far more in the east than in the west of England, where village squares had the same purpose.) The enclosure would have provided protection for the livestock in a wolf-infested country.*

The Saxons weren't the only colonisers of pre-Conquest England. New villages were also founded by the Scandinavian (Viking) settlers

*The Making of The English Landscape

in the 9th and 10th centuries. Some villages were taken over – for example, the Old English village of Northworthy, which became Derby. From place-names we can learn a great deal about the nature of the settlement (see chapter 7).

At Laxton (Notts) it's possible to see today the kind of open field landscape the Anglo-Saxons produced over much of the country. This is also perpetuated by the ridge-and-furrow, especially conspicuous in the Midlands. Villages were surrounded by two, or possibly three, large open fields (in contrast to the small, rectangular Celtic fields). The villagers ploughed their strips, which were separated from each other by a furrow. Ploughing threw the soil towards the centre of the strip, producing a high ridge. By the end of the Saxon period, England was far better cultivated than in Romano-British times, a fact partly explained by the heavy plough, possibly introduced by the (Danish) Vikings in the 9th or early 10th centuries. As in Roman England, there were watermills for grinding corn. Domesday (1086) records thousands. (Windmills didn't appear till the end of the 12th century.) For ceorls (free peasants) and thralls, the battles and power struggles of pre-Conquest England had little importance beside the heavy plough and watermill.

The Lord's Hall, where ale or mead was circulated in drinking horns, was a place of light and warmth on winter nights. In *Beowulf*, the Old English epic poem, the Hall described was 'lofty and high gabled ... strongly braced inside and out ... its high roof gilded, its mead benches decked in gold'. Its atmosphere contrasted with the cell in the monastery at Jarrow where the Venerable Bede (673–735) composed *A History of the English Church and People*. Bede, the finest historian in the Europe of his day, was mainly concerned to describe the most important event of the Anglo-Saxon period, namely the conversion of the English. The Hall figures in perhaps Bede's most famous passage – in 627 Edwin, King of Northumbria, dignified in the ASC by the title Bretwalda (Overlord of England), holds a council with his chief men about accepting the Faith of Christ. One of the councillors argues: 'Your Majesty, when we compare the present life of man with that time of which we have no knowledge, it seems to me like the swift flight of a lone sparrow through the banqueting-hall where you sit in the winter months to dine with your thanes and councellors. Inside there is a comforting fire to warm the room; outside the wintry storm of snow and rain are raging. This sparrow flies swiftly in through one door of the hall, and out through another. While he is inside, he is safe from the winter storms; but after a few moments of comfort, he vanishes from sight into darkness whence he came. Similarly, man appears on earth for a little while, but we know nothing of what went before this life, and what follows. Therefore if this new teaching can reveal any more certain knowledge, it seems only right that we should follow it.'

A later successor of Edwin, Oswald (also Bretwalda) sent for a Christian bishop, and Aidan duly arrive from Iona, the Hebridean island where Columba, an Irish expatriate, had established an evangelising monastic community. 'On Aidan's arrival, the King appointed the island of Lindisfarne to be his see as he asked. As the tide ebbs and flows, this place is surrounded by sea twice a day like an island, and twice a day the sand dries and joins it to the mainland.'

Aidan stayed with the Northumbrians until his death in 651. Lindisfarne, where he founded a monastery, was his base – a sort of power house for the conversion of northern England. When he wanted solitude, he retreated to Farne Island. 'Whether in town or country,' Bede also records, 'he always travelled on foot unless compelled by necessity to ride, and whenever he met anyone, whether high or low, he stopped and spoke to them. If they were heathen, he urged them to be baptized; and if they were Christians, he strengthened their faith, and inspired them by word and deed to live a good life and to be generous to others.'

For Bede Aidan fell short in one important respect – 'I greatly admire and love all these things about Aidan...but I cannot approve or commend his failure to observe Easter at the proper time....' Aidan, as a monk from Iona, was a Celtic Christian. Bede, on the other hand, was a monk in the Roman tradition.

The conversion of England took both Celtic and Roman forms. In 597 Augustine and his companions had arrived on the Isle of Thanet off the Kent coast. Ethelbert, the King of Kent, was a bit sceptical at first, but he did at length agree to meet Augustine. Almost certainly he was influenced by his Frankish wife, Bertha, who was already a Christian. The upshot of this historic confrontation on Thanet was a green light for the Roman conversion – 'The King,' writes Bede, 'then granted them a dwelling in the city of Canterbury, which was the chief city of all his realm, and in accordance with his promise, he allowed them provisions and did not withdraw their freedom to preach.' In this way Canterbury acquired the significance that Lindisfarne would soon assume in the north.

In the long run Roman traditions triumphed over Celtic ones, and Canterbury would be far more important. The chief argument, over the date of Easter, was settled in favour of Rome at a kind of summit conference in 664. This was convened by Oswy, the third of the great Bretwalda kings of Northumbria, and held in Abbess Hilda's mixed monastery high up on the cliff at Whitby. (The ruins of a later abbey church still stand impressively on this ancient site.) Oswy, the royal referee, gave the verdict. Bede records: 'All present, both high and low, signified their agreement with what the king had said, and abandoning their imperfect customs, readily accepted those which they had learned to be better.'

Bede died four years after completing his magnum opus. His 'heavenly birthday' (an expression he'd often used) occurred on 25 May 735, while he chanted, 'Glory be to the Father, and to the Son, and to the Holy Spirit,' on the floor of his cell. Cuthbert (not to be confused with the Sainted Abbot of Lindisfarne), pupil of Bede and future Abbot of Wearmouth and Jarrow, who witnessed the event, later wrote: 'And all who saw and heard of the death of our father Bede declared that they have never known anyone end his days in such deep devotion and peace.'

The market place at Wantage (Oxon) is overlooked by the statue of an Englishman as great in his own way as Bede – King Alfred.

Whitby Abbey (from south). It was founded in 657 by St. Hilda for monks and nuns. Hilda's abbey was destroyed by the Danes. This ruined abbey church dates mainly from the 12th and 13th centuries. (Chris Mountford)

49

Another statue is at Winchester, the capital of his Wessex kingdom, which became the first capital of England.

Alfred richly merits his statues because he prevented England's total absorption by the Vikings, an outcome threatening ever since (on June 8th 793) 'the harrying of the heathen miserably destroyed God's church on Lindisfarne by rapine and slaughter'.* However, his success against the Danes at Ashdown in Berkshire (871) – this was before he became king – when (according to the Anglo-Saxon Chronicle) he charged at the enemy 'like a wild boar' was not repeated. Later, following a successful Danish attack on his winter quarters at Chippenham, he retreated to Athelney (Somerset), then an island cut off by the marshes. Here he burned no cakes (an apocryphal 16th-century addition to Asser's Life of Alfred) but we know that he recruited an impressive force of fighting men. The famous Alfred Jewel, on display at the Ashmolean Museum in Oxford, was found near Athelney. Consisting of gold decorated with enamel, it bears the inscription, 'Aldred had me made'. The identity of the enamelled figure depicted will never be known.

In 878, Alfred's new force routed the Danes on the Wiltshire down above Edington (or Ethandun), fifteen miles to the south of the Danish camp at Chippenham. By the Peace of Wedmore (today a village with one of Somerset's loveliest church towers) the Danes gave up their attack on Wessex and agreed to a shotgun conversion. Like the Saxons before them, the invaders turned to colonisation. Many settled in the east midlands. The detailed Treaty of Wedmore (886) defined the boundaries of this Danish area (Danelaw). It included the Danish Kingdom of York, established by Halfdan in 876, and the Danish Five Boroughs of Derby, Leicester, Lincoln, Nottingham and Stamford, bases of Danish armies that colonised the surrounding territories in the post-Edington years. Alfred consolidated the English position by constructing coastal and inland burghs (centres fortified with a ditch and wooden palisade), for example at Hastings and Lewes (Sussex) and Oxford and Wallingford (by the Thames).

A scholar as well as a soldier, Alfred's translation (from Latin) of St. Gregory's *Pastoral Care* may be seen in the Bodleian Library at Oxford. Untypically for English monarchs, he would have been perfectly at home in the Bodleian. He had Bede's History translated, and possibly initiated the Anglo-Saxon Chronicle, that was written in English. With the Danes 'knocking on the door', it's remarkable that he achieved so much. Overwork may have contributed to his comparatively early death, at about 50, in 899.

*Anglo-Saxon Chronicle. Ed. G.N. Garmonsway (Everyman)

Mighty Alfred was not the first English ruler to claim authority over the whole country, nor was his dynasty the first to achieve that degree of importance. By about 600 a number of independent kingdoms had been established by the Anglo-Saxon settlers. The dynasties vied with each other – in the 7th century, the heathen Penda of Mercia twice killed Northumbrian Kings before being killed himself. At various time Ethelbert of Kent (who gave the all clear to Augustine), Raedwald of East Anglia (of Sutton Hoo fame), Edwin, Oswald and Oswy of Northumbria, and later Offa of Mercia (8th century) exercised overlordship. Of these only Offa wasn't actually designated 'Bretwalda' (Overlord) in the ASC, but he styled himself 'Rex Anglorum' and was possibly the most formidable ruler before Alfred, building his dyke to keep out the Welsh (in origin Celts chased west by the settling English) and introducing his silver pennies. Offa even had time to re-found a monastery at St. Albans. Following his death in 796, Mercia stayed supreme until defeated in 825 by Egbert of Wessex at the battle of Ellendun near Swindon. Then Mercia was overrun.

Egbert (reigned in Wessex 802–39) is often described as England's first King simply because his dynasty stayed at the helm. Credit for this is due, as we have seen, to Alfred, Egbert's grandson, but also to Athelstan, the grandson of Alfred (reigned 925–39) who in 927 smashed the Viking kingdom of York, then confirmed his supremacy ten years later at Brunanburh. The ASC entry for 938 celebrates this great victory, sited somewhere in the Midlands, with a poem:

> 'Never before in this island, as the books of ancient
> historians tell us, was an army
> Put to greater slaughter by the sword
> Since the time when Angles and Saxons landed,
> Invading Britain across the wide seas
> From the east, when warriors eager for fame,
> Proud forgers of war, the Welsh overcame,
> And won for themselves a kingdom.

The Edgar Window at Bath Abbey portrays the coronation in 973 of Edgar (reigned 949–75).

> 'In this year, Edgar, ruler of the English,
> Was consecrated king by a great assembly,
> In this ancient city of Acemannesceaster,
> Also called Bath by the inhabitants of this island.'

51

The ritual of the Anglo-Saxon coronation ceremony is the basis of modern cermonies. It included anointing with holy oil and chrism (oil and balsam mixed) and the taking of an oath. In 973 Edgar swore 'to maintain peace, to repress wrongdoing and to do justice with mercy' – the national monarchy inherited from the Saxons would carry with it a sense of obligation as well as of mystique. Also bequeathed were the royal household, that accompanied the King, and the occasional assembly, or Witan (literally 'the ones who know') from which the Post-Conquest council (Commune concilium) would evolve.

From Edgar's crowning at Bath to the battle of Hastings, the history of the Wessex (English) monarchy was distinctly chequered. Edgar only survived two years after his coronation. His son, Edward the Martyr, was assassinated when only 16 years of age at Corfe Castle (Dorset) by supporters of his stepbrother, Ethelred (reigned 979–1016). Ethelred, known as 'The Unraed' (The ill-advised), sensibly tried to pay off the Danes with his danegeld. Appeasement couldn't prevent the absorption of England into Cnut's Scandinavian empire, though the 'Englishness' of England was not submerged – the work of Alfred and Athelstan couldn't be easily undone.

This also held true after the Norman takeover in 1066. It could even be argued that in the long run the Normans were 'conquered' by the English – significantly, we speak an (essentially) pre-Conquest language that the Norman élite was eventually forced to learn. In some respects our England was almost 'made' by 1066. The framework of political unity had been established, as well as the organisation into shires, which has survived (despite the depredations of the Local Government Act of 1974!) This organisation was partly a Viking creation – four out of the five boroughs (Derby, Leicester, Lincoln and Nottingham) giving their names to Shires. The three Ridings (abolished in 1974) originated in the Scandinavian Kingdoms of York. In each shire the key official – well established by 1066 – was the sheriff (shire reeve) who presided over the shire court. He remained so until Tudor times, when the J.P's took over as chief preservers of the King's Peace in the localities.

The Anglo-Saxon legacy has many aspects, from Christianity to our (pre-decimalisation) coinage. The Saxon landscape of open arable fields would largely survive till the Agrarian Revolution of the 18th century. The wool trade would provide most of English wealth for centuries. The social principle of hierarchy – kings, earls, ceorls and thralls – was inherited and developed by the Normans – for example, the (unfree) thralls became the villeins. Even Feudalism, seen in the relationship of Saxon thegns ('servants') and their protecting lords, existed in embryo.

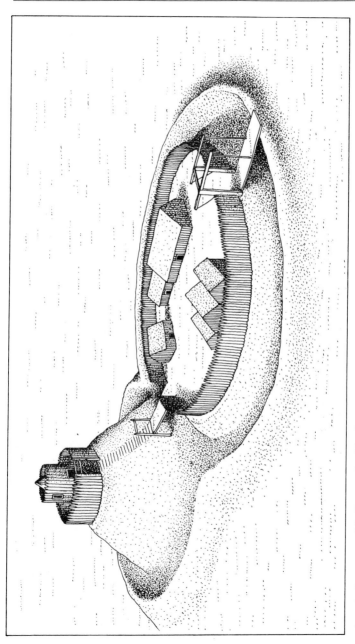

A typical motte and bailey castle. (David Cheepen)

'This was a fatal day for England, a melancholy havoc of our dear country'
William of Malmesbury

On a ridge above the Sussex town of Battle, the site of the most important engagement on English soil is marked by the ruins of a Benedictine abbey William vowed he would build in the event of victory. (In fact today's ruins are mainly those of the rebuilt 13th century monastery). Harold's death at Hastings was only the start of the Conquest, of which the castles the Normans built are the most powerful reminder. Initially they were built with timber, the material generally used in Anglo-Saxon architecture. The keep is situated on its motte (mound) on one edge of a large courtyard (bailey), both motte and bailey being enclosed by a ditch and palisade. Mountfichet Castle at Stansted (Essex) is a re-constructed motte and bailey castle, built on its original site.[*1] Stone castles, dominated by a square or cylindrical keep, started to be built in large numbers in the 12th century. The Norman keep was both a fortress and a place of residence, comprising a great hall and smaller rooms, often including a chapel. One of the first and best preserved was built (c.1140) by Aubrey de Vere at Hedingham, also in Essex[*2]

The remains of Colchester Castle. The huge keep was built on the foundations of the Roman temple. The temple's vaults may be visited. (Guildhall Library)

Scarborough Castle. The Norman keep, one of the finest in England, stands in the Inner Bailey. (Chris Mountford)

The 13th century saw the most spectacular developments in castle construction. The stimulus for these was the need to resist siege towers and battering rams. A perimeter (curtain) wall with towers was made to ring the keep and bailey. A pioneering example was at Framlingham in Suffolk. Warwick Castle's 14th-century curtain wall with its tower defences still magnificently survives. However, the best and most elaborate castles were mainly reserved for the Welsh!

Castles might strengthen royal power; in hostile hands, the reverse would be true. A strong king, such as the first Angevin, Henry II (1154–89), succeeding to the throne after the disorders engendered by Stephen and Matilda's disputed succession, knocked down some castles and took over others (including Warwick Castle's proud neighbour, Kenilworth). An incompetent king like Edward II (1307–27) or an arrogant one like Richard II (1377–99) were dispatched inside the castles of their enemies (Edward – most horribly – at Berkeley and Richard at Pontefract). Edward II's well preserved murder room at Berkeley Castle, overlooking the Severn, is a sombre reminder that kingly survival wasn't automatic in the no-

*[1]Open daily from March to November

*[2]Hedingham Castle is open daily May to October. An outing that combined both would make an instructive History lesson.

holds-barred world of baronial politics. Kings weren't absolute. If, like Richard II, they tried to act as though they were, their illusions were quickly dispelled! The practical constraints of this sacred office might also be brought home to the astute and powerful – the impressive Henry II, who extended royal justice to the whole country, was finally reduced to impotence by his rebellious sons. The youngest of these would later be confronted by his baronage at Runnymede – the most celebrated nemesis of a medieval king.

Gradually fewer castles were built, partly because the invention of gunpowder made them hard to protect (as, for example, the Lancastrian defenders of Bamburgh would find out during the Wars of the Roses). Castles might be harder to defend, but they could at least be made more comfortable. 14th century Bodiam Castle in East Sussex, partly designed at the outset for daily living, and whose hall and chapel can still be seen, reflects the narrowing divide between fortresses and great houses. The two 'merged' in the moated manor house, such as Ightam Mote, near Sevenoaks in Kent. For defensive purposes, the huge brick keep built in the mid-15th century at Tattershall Castle* (Lincs) was obsolete even at the outset.

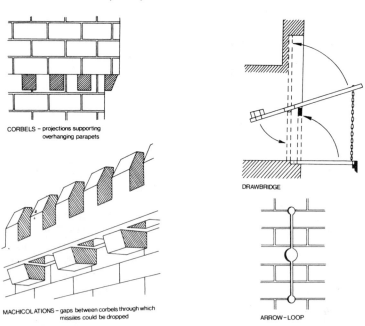

CORBELS – projections supporting overhanging parapets

MACHICOLATIONS – gaps between corbels through which missiles could be dropped

DRAWBRIDGE

ARROW–LOOP

Features of medieval castles (David Cheepen)

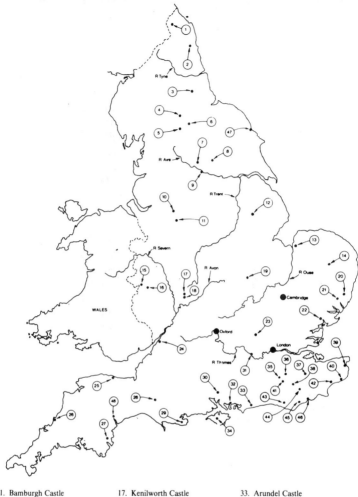

1. Bamburgh Castle	17. Kenilworth Castle	33. Arundel Castle
2. Alnwick Castle	18. Warwick Castle	34. Carisbrooke Castle
3. Durham Castle	19. Fotheringhay Castle	35. Hever Castle
4. Barnard Castle	20. Framlingham Castle	36. Ightam Mote
5. Bolton Castle	21. Burgh Castle	37. Leeds Castle
6. Richmond Castle	22. Colchester Castle	38. Scotney Castle
7. Clifford's Tower	23. Berkhamstead Castle	39. Richborough Castle
8. York Castle	24. Berkeley Castle	40. Dover Castle
9. Pontefract Castle	25. Dunster Castle	41. Penshurst Place
10. Peveril Castle	26. Tintagel Castle	42. Lympne Castle
11. Haddon Hall	27. Berry Pomeroy Castle	43. Lewes Castle
12. Lincoln Castle	28. Sherborne Old Castle	44. Bodiam Castle
13. Castle Rising	29. Corfe Castle	45. Pevensey Castle
14. Norwich Castle	30. Winchester Castle	46. Hastings Castle
15. Stokesay Castle	31. Windsor Castle	47. Scarborough Castle
16. Ludlow Castle	32. Portchester Castle	48. Exeter Castle

A map showing the location of medieval castles and moated manor houses.
David Cheepen

*N.T. Open daily March to October

The central feature of all castles and substantial houses was the hall. This was the main living-room and focus of the life of the household. The well-to-do yeoman or merchant had his 'hall house' which was very comfortable, though not so grand as the manor house. The hall reached up to the full height of the building for the central hearth required a high escape route for smoke to prevent the roof timbers catching fire. Even when wall fireplaces came in, lower ceilings didn't follow immediately. Some hall houses – extended and transformed – have survived the passage of time. This is not the case with thatched huts, built with simple frames, in which the labourers lived humbly and precariously.

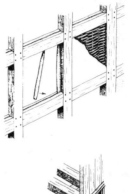

(i) Wattle and daub. (ii) Jetties and projecting windows.
(i) The spaces between the exposed timbers of medieval buildings were commonly filled in with wattles (often hazel) woven round upright staves. The wattle panel was then daubed on both sides with a mixture of clay, dung and straw. The finished panel was then limewashed or painted.
(ii) Jetties were an important feature of some timber-framed buildings. The upper wall jutted beyond the wall below, forming an overhang. A symbol of status, rather like cars in our day, the wealthy would want more than one – and the bigger the better! However, jetties were also practical, providing both extra floor space and protection from rain. (David Cheepen)

Wall painting at Chaldon Church, Surrey. Most medieval men and women learned about the Church's faith from pictures. This famous wall painting (c.1200) is a powerful sermon. The lower part portrays the torments of the wicked. At the foot of the ladder is a Symbol of Life. This may be gained by climbing the Ladder to Christ seated in glory. Top left – the Devil tries to weigh down St. Michael's scale with bad deeds. Top right – Christ transfixes the Devil with his victorious cross. (D. G. Hatton)

The precariousness of life was apparent to everyone – including kings. Edward II died at 43, Richard II at 33. Henry V only reached 35. Richard III bit the dust at 33. Because life was short and uncertain, men reached Heavenwards for fulfillment.

Medieval England's most durable legacy consists of churches and cathedrals. That few should have survived from the Anglo-Saxon period is chiefly attributable to Norman vandalism. The wooden church at Greensted, Essex (probably mid 9th century) has survived – against the odds. Both the tiny stone church at Bradford-on-Avon and the church at Brixworth (Northants), made with Roman bricks, invite pilgrimages.

The Norman Conquest hurried England into the architectural mainstream of the continent. The Normans were great church and cathedral builders, whose creations were allowed to last. Some of our greatest cathedrals – Durham, Ely, Norwich, St. Albans – are

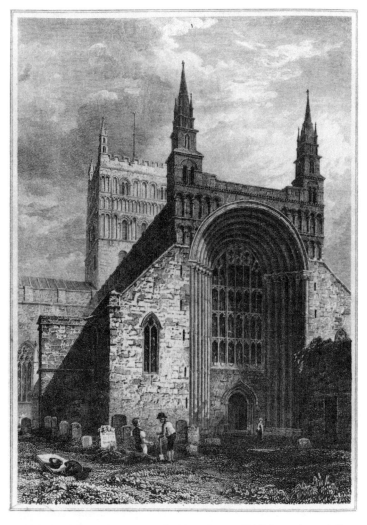

Tewkesbury Abbey. The Norman building (begun 1092) has substantially survived. (Guildhall Library)

essentially Norman (Romanesque). Round arches and thick pillars are obvious features. By the 13th century, in the wake of Angevin kings with extensive French territories, the Gothic style of pointed arches, slender pillars, large windows and tall spires had arrived from

1. Jarrow Priory
2. Carlisle Cathedral
3. Monkwearmouth Priory
4. Durham Cathedral
5. Whitby Abbey
6. Jervalux Abbey
7. Ripon Cathedral
8. Rievalux Abbey
9. Bolton Priory
10. Byland Abbey
11. Kirkham Priory
12. Kirkstall Abbey
13. Fountains Abbey
14. York Minister
15. Beverley Minister
16. Thornton Abbey
17. Rufford Abbey
18. Rufford Abbey
19. Lincoln Cathdral
20. Newstead Priory

21. Shrewsbury Abbey
22. Buildwas Abbey
23. Much Wenlock Abbey
24. Crowland Abbey
25. Peterborough Cathedral
26. Lichfield Cathedral
27. Worcester Cathedral
28. Hereford Cathedral
29. Walsingham Priory
30. Norwich Cathedral
31. Ely Cathedral
32. Bury St. Edmunds Cathedral
33. St. Albans Cathedral
34. Waltham Abbey
35. Evesham Abbey
36. Tewkesbury Abbey
37. Gloucester Cathedral
38. Bristol Cathedral
39. Malmesbury Abbey
40. Lacock Abbey

41. Bath Abbey
42. Wells Cathedral
43. Glastonbury Abbey
44. Sherborne Abbey
45. Salisbury Cathedral
46. Romsey Abbey
47. Winchester Cathedral
48. Waverley Abbey
49. Canterbury Cathedral
50. St. Augustine's Abbey
51. Battle Abbey
52. Lewes Priory
53. Arundel Priory
54. Chichester Cathedral
55. Beaulieu Abbey
56. Forde Abbey
57. Exeter Cathedral
58. Buckfast Abbey
59. Leiston Abbey
60. Furness Abbey
   (near Barrow-in-Furness)

A map showing the location of medieval cathedrals and religious houses (David Cheepen)

Kirkham Priory, Yorks, an Augustinian priory founded in 1122. This is the sculptured gatehouse. (Chris Mountford)

Rievaulx Abbey, the earliest of Yorkshire's Cistercian houses (founded 1132) (Chris Mountford)

France. Because very little stonework was used between the windows, flying (projecting) buttresses were built for support.

Salisbury Cathedral, begun in 1220, is a perfect example of this style. Being built in entirety from scratch, it possesses a unity that many cathedrals lack.

The Early English simplicity which Salisbury exemplifies was succeeded by the decorated phase, superbly illustrated by the vault of Exeter Cathedral. This was followed by the home-grown perpendicular style, marvellously represented by the choir of York Minster.

In the late summer of 1348, just thirteen years before work began on the choir of York Minster, a fateful cargo of flea infested rats arrived at the Dorset port of Melcombe Regis (now part of Weymouth). The Black Death reduced England's population by about one quarter, striking at the rich and powerful as well as the poor – of the three Archbishops of Canterbury in 1349, two died of the plague.

For surviving peasants the plague bacilli would prove a blessing in disguise. Because the labour supply was reduced, wages rose and

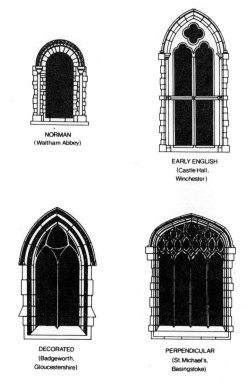

NORMAN
(Waltham Abbey)

EARLY ENGLISH
(Castle Hall,
Winchester)

DECORATED
(Badgeworth,
Gloucestershire)

PERPENDICULAR
(St. Michael's,
Basingstoke)

Medieval windows (David Cheepen)

holdings were easier to obtain. The villeins were encouraged to escape their manorial shackles and look for work and land. With the governing orders on the defensive, Parliament imposed the first wage freeze and tightened the seigneurial screws on peasants who remained unfree. Along with the infamous Poll Tax (universal and not graduated) this provided the fuel of the Peasants' Revolt of 1381.

The most famous revolt in English history originated in Kent and Essex. It ended up as a series of risings which, given the difficulty of communication, lacked co-ordination. Though mainly concentrated in the eastern counties, these were as far apart as York and Winchester. Targets were chiefly local centres of wealth and power – in St. Albans and Bury St. Edmunds, the abbeys, which were seen (with justification) as exploiting Landlords. In Cambridge it was the university, reflecting the perennial tension between Town and Gown. Temporary concessions might be exacted under duress, as they were

Worcester Cathedral. Built above the eastern bank of the R. Severn, this cathedral (mainly Early English) largely replaced the Romanesque building of the great Wulfston, a monk and prior of the monastery who later became Bishop of Worcester. The great Norman crypt still exists. King John, an admirer of Wulfston, is buried in the presbytery (the eastern part of the choir), (English Tourist Board)

J.Carter sculp!

Chichester Cathedral. The spire is a copy by Sir Gilbert Scott of the original (c.1400) which fell in 1861. (Guildhall Library)

from Thomas de la Mare, the eminent abbot of St. Albans, who stayed to negotiate while some of his monks fled.

The Establishment – better able to co-ordinate its efforts than the rebels – soon retaliated. The youthful Richard II himself arrived at St. Albans, where he supervised the trial (and hanging) of the local leaders. In East Anglia the revolt was crushed by the Bishop of Norwich. The Essex rebels were scattered at Billericay on 2nd July, marking the end of serious resistance.

On 25th July 1446, Henry VI laid the foundation stone of King's College Chapel. Prone to nervous breakdowns, the only child of Henry V preferred fine buildings to politics. Under a strong king, the Wars of the Roses would not have taken place. The wars were sustained by factors beyond his control – for example, the ability of barons to call out large armed followings provided the military resources of both Yorkists and Lancastrians. These retinues had a serving, feudal relationship with their lords, but one which did not involve the tenure of land (the distinguishing component of Norman

Beverley Minster

St. William's College, York. It was founded in 1461 to house the chantry priests attached to the Minster. (Chris Mountford)

feudalism). In fact it was similar to the 'Lordship' existing in Anglo-Saxon England – ie, of Harold in respect of his thegns. The monarch held the key, and if able to exert effective control, such 'affinities' made for social cohesion. If not, things got out of hand.... The Letters of the 'upwardly mobile' Paston Family of Norfolk provide abundant evidence that in their area this is what happened – and East Anglia was no exception. 'I was at Hellesdon upon Thursday last past,' wrote Margaret Paston in despair to her husband, John Paston, on 27 October 1465, 'and saw the place there, and in good faith there will no creature think how foul and horribly it is arrayed but if they saw it.' Not for the first or last time, one of their properties had been attacked. Later on their castle at Caister was seized by the Duke of Norfolk, a leading Yorkist. Two years after this, at the Battle of Barnet in 1471, the Paston fought on the Lancastrian side. This is one illustration of the way in which the local and the national conflicts were intertwined.

The first battle took place at St. Albans (1455) when the King was captured, and Edmund Beaufort, Duke of Somerset, his leading supporter, was killed. Following Richard, Duke of York's death at Wakefield (1460), the Yorkist claim was taken up by his son,

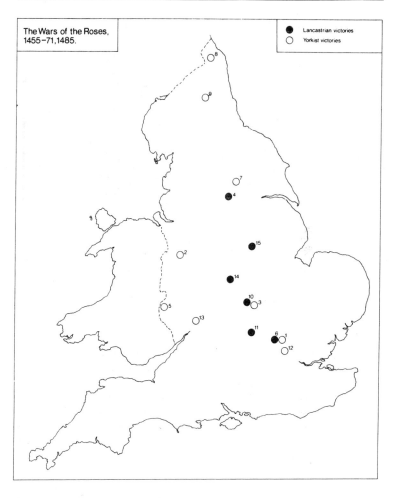

The Wars of the Roses, 1455–71, 1485.

● Lancastrian victories
○ Yorkist victories

1. St. Albans I, 1455
2. Blore Heath, 1459
3. Northampton I, 1460
4. Wakefield, 1460
5. Mortimer's Cross, 1461
6. St. Albans II, 1461

7. Towton, 1461
8. Hedgerley Moor, 1464
9. Hexham, 1468
10. Northampton II, 1468
11. Edgcott, 1469
12. Barnet, 1471

13. Tewkesbury, 1471
14. Bosworth Field, 1485
15. Stokefield 1487
   (The defeat of Lambert
   Simnel's rebellion)

Map showing the main battles of the Wars of the Roses (David Cheepen)

Edward, Earl of March (later Edward IV). His 'sponsor' was Richard Neville, Earl of Warwick, known as 'The Kingmaker'. In February 1461 Warwick was defeated by Margaret of Anjou, Henry's formidable queen, at the 2nd Battle of St. Albans. It was now, when the chips were down, that Edward snatched the throne. He then defeated Margaret's forces in a ten-hour battle in a snowstorm at Towton, three miles from Tadcaster (Yorks). She tried hard, but unavailingly, to regain her hold on the north. By 1464 Edward's position looked secure. Then it was temporarily destroyed by Warwick's defection to the Lancastrians. This was prompted by pique that Edward wouldn't do what he told him. The Kingmaker was even kept in the dark about Edward's marriage to the beautiful Elizabeth Woodville. Henry returned briefly to the throne in 1470, but the so-called Readeption ended in the thick fog at the battle of Barnet in April 1471, when Edward, back from exile, removed the Kingmaker for good. For the Lancastrians the disastrous sequel was at Tewkesbury, where Henry VI's only son, Prince Edward, was killed. 'It is a difficult matter to go out by the door and then try to come in by the window,' commented a contemporary, but Edward had achieved this feat. Once reinstalled, he set about reviving the wilting Monarchy. Less of a playboy King than has been imagined, the Tudors would reap the benefit from his constructive achievements.

South of Market Bosworth (Leics) a field overlooked by Ambien Hill, is the traditional site of the defeat of Richard III, younger brother of Edward IV, by Henry Richmond. The final outcome wasn't certain until the wavering Stanleys till then hedging their bets, threw in their lot with Richmond. Many others had hedged their bets by not turning up at all when the King mustered his troops at Leicester! It's possible that Richard lacked the ability to make men fight for him because child murderers were beyond the pale even in this endemically violent age. Richmond had no such difficulty. Thus the future lay with this uncompromised – and uncompromising – opponent, who went on to establish the most formidable dynasty England had seen.

Further Reading

In Search of the Dark Ages Michael Wood (B.B.C., 1981)

A History of the English Church and People Bede (Penguin, revised edition 1968)

Anglo-Saxon England F.M. Stenton (Oxford, 1947)

The Beginnings of English Society D. Whitelock (Penguin, 1952)

The Monastic Order in England M.D. Knowles (Cambridge, 2nd edition 1963)

The Religious Orders in England M.O. Knowles (Cambridge, 3 vols, 1948–59)

The Feudal Kingdom of England F. Barlow (Longman, 1955)

Angevin Kingship J.E.A. Jolliffe (Black, 2nd edition 1963)

The Black Death Philip Ziegler (Collins, 1969)

Medieval People E. Power (Methuen, 10th edition 1963)

Deserted Medieval Villages M.W. Beresford (Lutterworth, 1971)

The Plantaganets John Harvey (Fontana, 1967)

The Wars of the Roses John Gillingham (Weidenfeld and Nicholson, 1981)

7 Historic England (3)

The Quest for King Arthur

The evidence for Arthur's existence is sketchily based on Nennius' *History of the Britons*, c.830. Gildas' 6th-century account of Romano-British resistance to the Saxons makes no mention of him at all. However, Gildas records a short-term British success at Mount Badon, which would have taken place in the 490s. Nennius attributes this victory to Arthur. Since he is virtually impossible to rescue from the mists of time, we are left with guesswork and tradition, which either faith or ignorance can invest with historicity.

Two-and-a-half miles north-west of Wimborne Minster (Dorset) lie **Badbury Rings**, a hill-fort commanding a marvellously unspoiled view. This is one suggested site of the battle of Mount Badon. Another is Liddington Castle, a hill-fort near Swindon (Wilts).

Of the many sites with alleged Arthurian associations, none is more romantic than **Tintagel** (N. Cornwall), the supposed birthplace. Historically, Tintagel was the location of a Celtic monastery that predated the Battle of Mount Badon. By comparison, the ruined castle is relatively recent in origin, for it dates from the 12th century.

Cadbury Castle (Somerset, 12 miles south-east of Glastonbury), an Iron Age hill-fort defended by four and, in places, five ramparts, with ditches between them, is the suggested site of Camelot. Historically, Ethelred the Unready established a royal mint here, later destroyed by his Scandinavian successor, Cnut.

Glastonbury (originally an island rising above the marshes) has been identified with Avalon. It was the 'spiritual capital' – if Camelot was the Arthurian equivalent of London, Avalon was akin to Canterbury.

In front of the High Altar of the ruined Abbey church, King Arthur's and Queen Guinevere's bones allegedly lie buried. Beneath Glastonbury Tor about one mile east of the town, tradition says that Joseph of Arimathaea buried the Holy Grail (the chalice used by Christ at the Last Supper) which was found in the end by Galahad. When Joseph drove his staff into the earth, it took root to produce the first Glastonbury thorn. The Tor is surmounted by the tower of the medieval **Chapel of St. Michael**. At its foot there is a bubbling spring called the **Chalice Well**.

By decorating the so-called **Round Table** in the hall of **Winchester Castle** with a Tudor Rose, Henry VII demonstrated the Welsh Tudors' powerfully propagandist claim to descent from the shadowy British Chieftain – an instance of legend helping to shape the historical process.

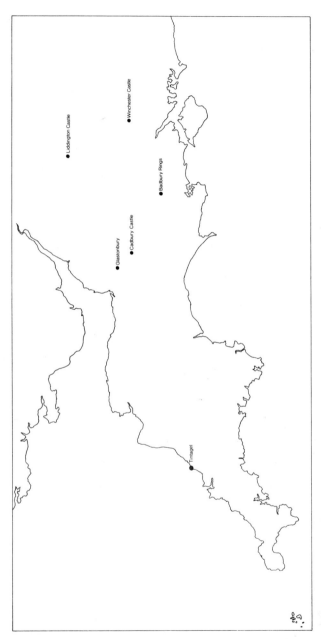

Places associated with King Arthur (David Cheepen)

Glastonbury Tor (David Cheepen)

The Annals of Wales, a source roughly contemporaneous with Nennius, refer to both the Battle of Badon and to 'The Fight at Camlann in which Arthur and Medraut (Mordred) were killed'. 'Camlann' may well be a late form of 'Camboglanna', the Roman name of the fort of Birdoswald on Hadrian's Wall near Carlisle. This philological clue has prompted speculation that Arthur, if he existed at all, was not a Dark Age 'freedom fighter' in the south-west, mobilising British resistance to the Saxon invader, but a British chief in the Solway region engaged in some internecine conflict with a British rival, the precise cause and nature of which the Mists of Time will forever conceal.

Glastonbury

Mystery and legend have tended to overlay the genuine historical interest of Glastonbury where, in the 10th century, the abbey was the most important monastic house in England. This position was due to Dunstan (901–88), the greatest English churchman of his age, who received his early education here from the monks. After a spell at court, he returned to Glastonbury as abbot, then masterminded the 10th century church reform, 'so that all this English land was filled with his holy teaching'. (Memorials of St. Dunstan.)

The present abbey ruins date from the late 12th century, when rebuilding began after a fire had destroyed the buildings St. Dunstan would have known. Don't miss the **Abbot's Kitchen**, one of the most completely preserved medieval kitchens in Europe. The monastic gatehouse has a small museum containing a model of the abbey as it was on the eve of its dissolution in 1539.

The Abbot's Kitchen, Glastonbury Abbey (David Cheepen)

Holy Island

Aidan's abbey was destroyed by the Vikings in 793. The present remains are of an 11th-century priory, begun for the Benedictines of Durham. In the wake of dissolution, the mid-16th-century castle, designed as a defence against the Scots, was built with stone from the priory ruins. The castle itself was a ruin from the Civil War to the start of the present century, when a pleasing restoration was carried out by Sir Edwin Lutyens.

Offa's Dyke

Offa of Mercia built his dyke to keep out the Welsh. This remarkable feat of engineering was a wonder of the Saxon world. The defensive bank, going from the Dee estuary (at the north end) to the mouth of the River Wye, was topped by a wooden palisade with stonework. To the east, and roughly parallel, is a shorter (and probably older) earthwork called **Wat's Dyke**.

Viking York

A centre of learning before the rise of Oxford and Cambridge, the great figure of York's pre-Viking era was a Yorkshireman named Alcuin, who left for Aachen in 782 to run Charlemagne's palace school.

When in 867 York was captured by the Danes, the Viking kingdom of York was established, and the city was transformed into a prosperous commercial centre.

In the 10th century Norse kings held sway. When the last of these, Eric Bloodaxe, died in battle on Stainmore (Westmorland) in 954, the kingdom became a shire, though preserving the Scandinavian division into ridings.

The **Coppergate** site yielded a treasure trove of finds – including the well-preserved remains of houses and workshops – now permanently and imaginatively displayed at the Jorvik Viking Centre, a marvellous recreation of the wealthy, bustling town.

Winchester

The Anglo-Saxon Chronicle records that 'in this year (648) was built the church at Winchester which king Cenwalh had made and

77

Offa's Dyke (David Cheepen)

consecrated in St. Peter's name.' This reference is to Old Minster, where, in the 8th century, Bishop Swithun had his seat. When, on 15th July 971, his remains were to be translated from outside to a golden shrine within the church, it is supposed to have rained for 40 days, so delaying the removal. By this time, an abbey, known as New Minster, had been built to the north of the Old Minster.

Both cathedral and abbey were worthy of Winchester's 10th and 11th century status as capital of Wessex and England, an administrative pre-eminence only gradually surrendered to London in the post-Conquest period. The largest town south of the Thames, its population in 1086 was probably c.6000, and this was less than 20 years before.

Nothing of Old Minster may be seen today. Perhaps not wishing the English to be reminded of past glories, the Normans efficiently erased all the great churches of the Saxon state. In this respect, few dictators of our century have shown such single minded zeal as the Conqueror.

In the present cathedral (the longest in England) the Norman work is best preserved in the **transepts**. In the 13th century the church was enlarged at the eastern end by the **Lady Chapel**. The episcopacy of William of Wykeham (1366–1404), founder of Winchester College (and New College, Oxford) saw extensive remodelling. In this period the Norman nave was cased in perpendicular stonework

The remains of the originally Norman castle are at the west end of the town. The **Great Hall** (1235) in the Early English style, where the (14th century) Round Table hangs, is said to be the finest in England after Westminister.

Domesday 1086*

This mammoth survey was launched at the Conqueror's Christmas court in 1085, in the twilight of his reign. Its precise purposes have been debated, but this does not diminish its value as a source of comprehensive information about 11th-century England. Her population was c.1½ million (probably over 2 million *less* than in Roman times). In contrast to highly populated areas like East Anglia and Kent, there were huge forests (enclosed parks for hunting), notably the New Forest, William's own creation. 80% of the area cultivated in 1914 was already under the plough. 6000 mills are recorded, all driven by water power. There were potteries and quarries and in Cheshire a salt industry. Iron was extracted and forged. However, the basis of England's wealth – as it would long remain – was wool. *N.B. Northumberland and Durham are omitted by the survey, and also London, Winchester and some other towns.*

*See *Domesday. A Search for The Roots of England*, Michael Wood (BBC Publications) 1986.

A SPECIMEN ENTRY

The Abbot of Ely holds HATFIELD. It answers for 40 hides. Land for 30 ploughs. In Lordship 20 hides; 2 ploughs there; a further 3 possible.

A priest with 18 villages and 18 smallholders have 20 ploughs; a further 5 ploughs possible. 12 Cottagers; 6 slaves.

4 mills at 47s 4d; meadow for 10 ploughs; pasture for the livestock; woodland, 2000 pigs; from the customary dues of the woodland and pasture, 10s.

The total value is and was £25; before 1066 £30.

This manor lay and lies in the Lordship of the Church of Ely.

The Domesday Book is preserved in 2 volumes at the Public Record Office, London.

Four Cathedrals – St. Albans, Durham, Ely and Norwich.

St. Albans

It is the St. Albans tradition that the abbey was founded by King Offa in 793. However, Bede records in his 'Ecclesiastical History' that 'when peaceful Christian times returned (i.e. after the persecution in which Alban died), a church (ecclesia) of wonderful workmanship was built, a worthy memorial of his martyrdom. To this day sick people are healed in this place and the working of frequent miracles continues to bring it renown.'

When taken with statements from earlier centuries, we have 'evidence as clear and as consistent as could possibly be expected for the continued existence of a cult of St. Alban centred on a church of Roman origin built on or near the site or sites of his martyrdom and burial'.[1]

It would therefore appear that Offa rebuilt an already existing church and reformed under a Benedictine rule an existing community. St. Albans historians 'by inflating Offa's role, effectively denied to their house its claim to an antiquity surpassing that of any other in the land'.[2]

[1], [2] 'Alban and the Anglo-Saxon Church', Martin Biddle. (From 'Cathedral and City. St. Albans ancient and modern', Martyn Associates, 1977).

St. Albans Cathedral (Chris Mountford)

From 1077 the Anglo-Saxon church was systematically demolished by Paul of Caen in order to make way for the Romanesque abbey church, the core of the building we see today. This process is likely to have paralleled the rebuilding at Winchester, where a start was made at the east end clear of the existing church, the destruction of Old Minster taking place as the new church was extended westwards.

St. Albans became the premier abbey in England. Twenty miles along Watling Street from London, the high and mighty found it convenient to stay here – there were 300 stabling places for visitors' horses. In this way Matthew Paris, the 13th-century monk/historian/artist/cartographer, whose lively chronicling illuminates his age, got to know Henry III. There was a great complex of monastic buildings. Apart from the church, the gatehouse, built by Thomas de la Mare, has survived. The modern chapter house (1982) occupies the site of the original chapter house.

The bricks for the abbey church were collected by Saxon and Norman builders from Verulamium – they are twice as old as the abbey itself. Inside they were covered with plaster, which was

81

Wall painting, St. Albans Cathedral (Chris Mountford)

Reredos, St. Albans Cathedral (Chris Mountford)

painted. In recent years many of the wall paintings (which once made St. Albans famous) have been uncovered. Find **Thomas Becket**, an unpopular figure in reformers' eyes. They scratched out his face.

Spot the **pillars** in the **Triforium** of the **South Transept** – the only bits of the Saxon church to be used by the Normans.

The glory of this abbey is the 15-century **reredos** (screen) behind the High Altar. Look, among the carved figures, for a Pope. This is Nicholas Breakspear, a spectacular case of a local boy coming good. His father became a monk here. It is said that the monastery once turned down his son. The **Nave** is the longest in England. West of the damaged nave screen, five bays of decorated Gothic on the south side face five Romanesque bays, which the south five bays had originally matched. When they collapsed, rebuilding under the Abbot, Richard of Wallingford (who was more interested in astronomical clocks) took such a long time that the style was changed.

The church was restored in the 19th century by Lord Grimthorpe. Like Richard of Wallingford, Grimthorpe was fond of clocks – he helped to design Big Ben. Though uniformity can be dull, his neo-Gothic additions are generally thought to detract from the essentially Romanesque building. The **Bankers Window** in the North

Durham Cathedral (Guildhall Library)

transept, with its circular shapes of glass corresponding to the size of coins, is an apposite memorial to the wealthy horologist.

The *raison d'être* of this building was the once brightly painted **Shrine** of St. Alban – a little paint can still be seen. The pedestal of Purbeck marble is covered with carvings of scenes from the martyrdom. The shrine was guarded from the watching chamber beyond.

A delightful story is told that, when Vikings threatened, the monks overtly sent the precious bones to Ely for safe keeping. When it was time to return them, the monks of Ely, delighted with their acquisition, substituted false ones. In fact, they had been given false bones!

Remember to light a candle by the shrine.

Durham

Cathedral and castle stand on a great rock, three-quarters moated by the River Wear. Very little of the castle survives from the Norman period. The cathedral contrastingly is 'the incomparable masterpiece of Romanesque architecture' (*The Cathedrals of England* Alex Clifton Taylor, Thames & Hudson).

Altar screen, Durham Cathedral. The pinnacled stone screen, dating from 1372 to 80, was a gift of John, Lord Neville. (Chris Mountford)

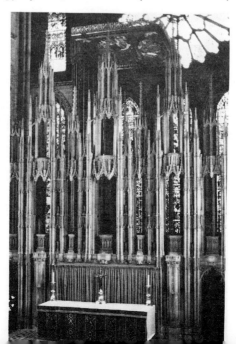

The foundation stones of the present cathedral (the first to be rib-vaulted) were laid on 11 August 1093. By 1099 the chancel, apses, crossing and transept were almost finished. The nave was complete by 1133. The **Chapel of the Nine Altars** at the east end belongs to a significantly later period. It was planned by Richard le Poore, previously Bishop of Salisbury, in the Early English style of his former cathedral.

In 1104 the body of St. Cuthbert (633–87) was transferred from the cloister to the east end. Essentially, the cathedral is Cuthbert's resting place. His shrine, made of green marble and gilded with gold, was one of England's richest monuments. Medieval religion could be theatrical, as well as colourful. On 20 March (St. Cuthbert's Day), and other special occasions, the raising of the shrine's oak cover by a pulley system – the pulley fixed in the vault, and silver bells attached to the rope – was an impressive spectacle for the thronging pilgrims. A simple **tomb** remains. At the west end, in the **Galilee Chapel,** is the **Tomb of the Venerable Bede**.

12th cent. Sanctuary knocker, North Porch, Durham Cathedral. '... the abbey church and all the churchyard and the circuit thereof was a sanctuary for all manner of men that had done or committed any great offence...' The
Rites of Durham
(Anon) Late 16th century.
(This is a replica. The original is displayed in the Treasury) (Chris Mountford)

Ely

In the marshy fenland Hereward 'the last of the English' fought his guerrilla campaign against the Normans. Around this time the present structure was begun (1083). Clifton-Taylor considered the **West Front** the finest of the Norman facades.

The magnificent Norman nave has survived but the Norman crossing tower did not – hence the unique 14th-century octagonal tower surmounting a timber vault carrying an octagonal lantern, 800 tons of lead and timber apparently hanging in space.

Norwich

The city of Norwich, overlooked by Henry I's greatly restored **Norman Keep**, is redolent of the Middle Ages. In **Strangers' Hall**, the 15th century hall of a merchant's house, or walking up cobbled **Elm Hill**, it's not hard to envisage the medieval town, with its bustle and odours – as well as its omnipresent piety. The city had expanded fast because there were no Roman walls to inhibit the growth (the Romans' town was Caister).

The cathedral has changed little from Norman times, when it was built by Bishop Losinga. He rebuilt much of the town at the same time (though the irregular Anglo-Saxon street plan has been preserved).

The spire surmounting the Norman tower dates from the 15th century. The vaulted roof and the choirstalls, with their misericords, belong to the same period.

The **Monk's Door** and the **Prior's Door** lead from the south aisle to the **Cloisters**, the only example of a two-storeyed monastic cloister in England (rebuilt 1297–1425). Admire the **vault-bosses** and the **tracery** of the cloister windows. On the east side the Decorated entrance still survives of the long gone Chapter-house.

The White Monks in England

In 1135 a handful of monks wishing to observe the rule more strictly walked out of the Benedictine abbey of St. Mary's, York and settled in wooden huts on the Archbishop of York's estates in Skeldale, near Ripon. This was the inauspicious start of Fountains Abbey, whose monks belonged to the Cistercian (White Monk) order, begun at Citeaux (S. France) in 1098, which especially flourished in York-

Norwich Cathedral (David Cheepen)

Fountains Abbey (Chris Mountford)

shire. The ruins of **Rievaulx Abbey** (near Helmsley) are as magnificent as those at Fountains.

Hard manual labour was an essential requirement of Cistercian communities. To bear the brunt a class of lay-brothers (conversi) was recruited. At Rievaulx there were five hundred in 1167 (but only 140 choir monks). Gangs of conversi in rotation would spend weeks out on granges (ranches). The English Cistercians were the frontiersmen of medieval England – the great colonisers of marginal land (woodland, marsh and fen). Even whole villages were wiped out in the cause of establishing their granges. No wonder there was a contemporary saying that the whole earth was becoming Cistercian.

Ashwell

Towns decline and fall like empires. Perhaps the most spectacular example is Dunwich (Suffolk), a leading port of medieval England, now mainly submerged.* In 1806 Ashwell, astride the Icknield Way, on the northern edge of Hertfordshire, was a thriving market town, mentioned in Domesday as one of the five boroughs of Herts along with Hertford, Stanstead Abbots, Berkhamsted and St. Albans. But

*See *Men of Dunwich* Rowland Parker (Collins).

in the end the competition of rising Baldock and Royston would prove too strong.

Today Ashwell is rich in timber-framed reminders of its more glorious past – such as the **Town House** (early Tudor) now a village Museum. On the walls of the **14th-Century Church**, whose **tower** is a striking landmark for miles around, can be seen **Graffiti**, including one of Old St. Paul's, dating back to the Black Death.

Canterbury

St. Augustine's arrival in 597 led to the founding of the first cathedral of Christ Church (of which nothing has survived). Canterbury became the metropolitan city of the English church. The Normans rebuilt the cathedral (with the largest crypt in England) and built a castle now in ruins. In 1170 Thomas Becket was murdered here – the greatest coup of all, Canterbury immediately becoming a European centre of pilgrimage.

Following the disastrous fire of 1174, William of Sens, the French master mason, designed the CHOIR and APSE in the Gothic style (the earliest example in England). This William didn't complete the job because he fell from scaffolding, so it was finished by another

Canterbury Cathedral (Guildhall Library)

William, an English mason. Two hundred years later, the perpendicular **Nave** was designed by the great Henry Yevele, of Westminster Hall fame. Dominating the exterior, the **Bell Harry Tower** dates from the late 15th century. The glass is magnificent, perhaps finer than at any other cathedral, even York Minster. **Trinity Chapel**, on the south side of the cathedral, contains the spendid tombs of the Black Prince (died 1376) and Henry IV (Bolingbroke), who died in 1413, and his queen. It was the Black Prince who provided the **stone screens** for the **Chapel of Our Lady** in the Norman crypt.

Apart from the cathedral, Canterbury is rich in medieval reminders: the surviving **town walls**, including the **West Gate** (probably Yevele's), the **Norman staircase** at the King's School, the ruins of **St. Augustine's Abbey** (which once rivalled Christ Church Priory), **St. Martin's Chruch**, built by King Ethelbert for Queen Bertha before St. Augustine arrived, **Greyfriars**, part of the first Franciscan friary in England, the **Refectory** and **Undercroft** of **Blackfriars**, and the 14th century buildings of the **Poor Priests' Hospital**.

Runnymede 1215

Medieval kings could fall foul of their subjects by either gross incompetence or excessive efficiency. John (1199–1216) was the youngest son of Henry II. All medieval kings moved around, but John was more restlessly peripatetic than any other, and everywhere the barons came under the lash of his financial demands. His very success at squeezing the feudal lemon till the pips squeaked produced a baronial reaction.

On the level meadow by the Thames knowns as Runnymede, the barons, reinforced by the Archbishop of Canterbury, forced John to seal the Magna Carta. This placed indelibly on record that the King's power was subject to the rule of Law. 'No freeman,' stated Article 39, 'shall be arrested or imprisoned or deprived of his freehold or outlawed or banished or in any way ruined, nor will we take or order action against him except by the lawful judgment of his equals and according to the law of the land.'

Four original copies of the Magna Carta exist, one each in Salisbury and Lincoln Cathedrals, and two in the British Museum.

Corfe Castle (David Cheepen)

Six Castles – Corfe, Windsor, Ludlow, Dover, Leeds and Alnwick

Corfe

At the gate of the Saxon Corfe Castle (a timbered stronghold) King Edward the Martyr was murdered by Ethelred's supporters (978). Today's hilltop ruins – once seen never forgotten – are mainly Norman.

Windsor

A hill by the Thames was a natural location for one of the Conqueror's timbered motte-and-bailey castles. Stonework followed. The **Round Tower** was built by Henry II. By the end of Henry III's reign (1272), the defences were substantially those we see today. England's largest castle, with its two baileys, was ideally placed to guard this approach to London.

Edward III (reigned 1327–77) was born here, loved the place, and founded The Order of the Garter, with its own chapel, in 1348. The

Windsor Castle (Guildhall Library)

Chapel we see today, dedicated to St. George, the Order's patron saint, was begun in 1478 for Edward IV. In the perfection of its perpendicular style, this burial place of royalty ranks with King's College Chapel.

Ludlow

Overmighty subjects could operate from the Welsh marches with impunity. From his base at Ludlow Roger Mortimer conspired with Queen Isabella against Edward II. When Yorkist and Tudor monarchs took control of the turbulent region, the castle became the seat of their representative, the Lord President of the Marches.

The Norman **Keep, Round Chapel** and **Curtain Wall** are the oldest parts of Ludlow Castle, one of the few to be built in stone from the start. In this period it was confined to what is now the Inner Bailey (or Ward). Inside the Norman curtain, Mortimer built a small palace, comprising the **Solar** (a lord's private quarters off the hall), **Great Hall, Great Chamber** and **King's Chamber**. One's imagination must invest these palatial ruins with the magnificence befitting the magnate who dispatched Edward II.

Dover

Dover Castle is one of the earliest concentric castles in England. The **Keep** was built in the 1180's in the middle of an inner ward (bailey). The curtain wall of the surrounding outer bailey was begun soon after. Just twenty one miles separating Dover from the continent, the castle was (in a chronicler's words) the 'Key of England'.

With Hastings, Romney, Hythe and Sandwich, Dover was one of the original Cinque ports (later joined by Winchelsea and Rye) granted the profits of justice in return for providing ships for the King's service. The Warden of the Cinque Ports, whom the king appointed, was also constable of Dover Castle.

Leeds

This idyllically moated castle, sited on two islands, and dating from the 12th century, was acquired in 1272 by Edward I for his beloved Queen Eleanor. Royal ownership continued until the reign of Henry VIII who, with his typical profligacy, gave it away.

Dover Castle (Guildhall Library)

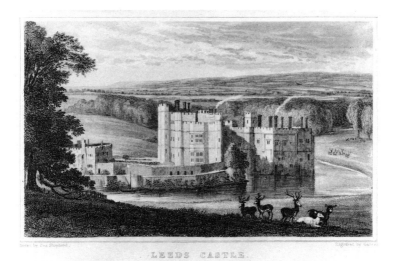

LEEDS CASTLE.
KENT.

Leeds Castle (Guildhall Library)

95

The Barbican, Alnwick Castle (Chris Mountford)

Alnwick

One of the marvellous series of Northumbrian castles – **Warkworth, Dunstanburgh** and **Bamburgh** are others – in 1309 Alnwick Castle became the property of the Percies, the most powerful family in the north. They have the hearts of the people by north and ever had, commented a 15th-century writer. Even in Tudor times it was said that the north had never known a king other than a Percy, a Neville or a Dacre (all northern families). Thus Monarchs could only control the Marches with Percy co-operation, and this could never be counted upon. Secure in their great strongholds, of which Warkworth to the south is a fine, less restored, example, the Percies dared to be disloyal. At Warkworth in 1403 the first Percy Earl of Northumberland and his son Harry Hotspur planned their famous rebellion against Henry IV. This culminated in Hotspur's death at the Battle of Shrewsbury.

Alnwick Castle, with its huge keep, is almost wholly a Percy creation. Large portions date from the 14th century. A fortress in themselves, the **Barbican** and **Gatehouse**, through which one enters the outer bailey, were built in the 15th century by the 2nd Earl of Northumberland, son of the ill-fated Hotspur. Much, however, is the product of 18th- and 19th-century restoration – if your taste is for romantic ruins, Dunstanburgh, or Warkworth, will have the stronger appeal.

The grounds were laid out in the 18th century by Capability Brown.

Dunstanburgh Castle (Chris Mountford)

The Lion Tower, Warkworth Castle (Chris Mountford)

Bamburgh Castle (Chris Mountford)

Fortified Manor Houses – Stokesay Castle and Ightam Mote

Stokesay Castle

This is a fortified manor house in an attractive Salopian setting. Barely defensible, its very existence suggests that, at the end of the 13th century, even on the Welsh Marches, life was rather more peaceful and settled than it had been. The Moat is dry. One enters through a half-timbered **Gatehouse** (16c), that replaced the original stone defensive gatehouse. There are two **Towers (North** and **South)**, both begun in the 13th century and a **Great Hall** and **Solar** (begun c.1285). In the hall spot the **hearth** – a rare 13th century survival – and the blackened roof timbers above.

99

Stokesay Castle (Guildhall Library)

Ightam Mote (English Tourist Board)

Ightam Mote

A moated gem of a building – hard to find being tucked away in the Kent countryside, but well worth the effort! The wings of the house surround a large, square courtyard, the Tudor wing, with its vertical, close-spaced timbers, perfectly complementing the medieval stonework. The **Gatehouse** and **Great Hall** were built in the 14th century. The domestic **Chapel** belongs to the Tudor period.

Bodiam Castle

When, during the 100 Years War, Richard II was prompted by French raids on the south coast to instruct Sir Edward Dalyngrigge to 'strengthen and crenellate' his manor house at Bodiam, Sir Edward chose to build a castle (1386–8).

The traditional keep is replaced by a rectangular courtyard guarded by a huge **Gatehouse** – two rectangular towers united by an arch crowned with a parapet. A moat surrounds the outer walls. Though occasioned by military necessity, the domestic arrangements are not incidental, as had been the case with the early castles – in this respect, Bodiam resembles a fortified manor house like Ightam Mote.

Bodiam Castle—South Side.

Bodiam Castle (Guildhall Library)

Haddon Hall

This wonderfully preserved medieval house is situated on a slope above the Wye. The ground floor Hall, dividing the two courtyards, dates from the early 14th century.

Haddon Hall (English Tourist Board)

Old Sarum and Salisbury

A hill north-west of Salisbury is the site of an ancient settlement going back to the Iron Age (from which the outer bank dates). Old Sarum's location at the crossing of important roads ensured

102

successive occupation by Romans (Sorviodunum), Saxons and the Normans. Round the Norman fortress, now marked by a mound, a small town drew up, including a cathedral. In the early 13th century, the hilltop was abandoned for the more sheltered Avon valley below. To this new site the see of Old Sarum was duly transferred.

The – second – cathedral was consecrated in 1258, building having begun 38 years previously under the direction of Bishop Poore. The decorated **Cloisters** – the largest in any English cathedral – were built between 1263 and 70. The beautiful spire (the highest in England) was added in the 14th century. The keen observer will spot that the apex (404 feet) is visibly ($2\frac{1}{2}$ feet) out of perpendicular.

Salisbury Cathedral (Guildhall Library)

The appeal of the interior is the satisfying uniformity of its Early English style. For some, however, the lack of variety is a drawback. Old glass is largely absent, so be sure to appreciate the (medieval) grisaille (greyish-white with monochrome decoration) – for example, in the **Lady Chapel** at the east end. The horologically inclined will be intrigued by the oldest surviving clock mechanism in Europe (1386).

Richard Le Poore – like Norwich's Bishop Losinga – was a town

103

planner. He laid out the city to the north of the cathedral on a grid-iron plan, with straight streets cutting the site into rectangles, inside which house-plots were marked out, each one paying a yearly ground rent to the bishop. The market-place was located with the guildhall on one side and the chief parish church on the other. Bishop Poore's 13th century plan has survived to this day, and it forms the nucleus of modern Salisbury.

Chester and York – Walls and Streets

It takes under an hour to walk round the medieval (and Roman) wall that once protected Chester. The six sections (going anti-clockwise) are:

1. New Gate to East Gate
2. East Gate to King Charles Tower
3. King Charles Tower over North Gate to Water Tower
4. Water Tower to Grosvenor Road
5. Grosvenor Road by the Castle to Bridge Gate
6. Bridge Gate to New Gate

BISHOP LLOYDS HOUSE, WATERGATE ST CHESTER. A.D. 1615

The Rows, Chester (Guildhall Library)

Micklegate Bar, York (Chris Mountford)

The Shambles, York (Chris Mountford)

The most important of the gates (for Watling Street) was East Gate. Close by is the **Cathedal**, once an abbey church. Some monastic buildings have magnificently survived on the north side, round the cloister. Of these the 13th-century **Refectory** must not be missed. The balconied **Rows**, on both sides of **Eastgate, Bridge** and **Watergate** streets could be as old as the Mystery Plays, which – preceding York's – originated in the Abbey c.1375. Plan to shop in the Rows on a Saturday, when the city centre's atmosphere is unforgettably vibrant.

York's encircling wall may also be walked round. **Monk Bar, Walmgate, Micklegate** and **Bootham Bar** were the four main gates. With its overhanging frontages, the **Shambles** exemplifies the narrow, twisting streets of a medieval town.

Merton College Oxford*

Matthew Arnold's 'city of dreaming spires' receives a mention in the Anglo-Saxon Chronicle (for 912) – a town was here long before the gown! By the 13th century, the reputation of England's first university, comprising a small number of corporate bodies (colleges) for clerics, was 'rivalling Paris's'.

Merton College Library (Guildhall Library)

Of the oldest colleges, all with 13th century endowments (**University College, Balliol, Merton** and **St. Edmund Hall**) Merton's medieval heritage is physically the best preserved. Take a stroll in Mob Quad, Oxford's oldest quadrangle. The naveless **Chapel** has a traceried east window of original 13th-century stained glass. The perpendicular tower dates from the 15th century. The 14th-century **Library** (over a century older than the Bodleian) is situated on the south-west corner of the Quad.

*See *Oxford* Jan Morris (OUP) 1987

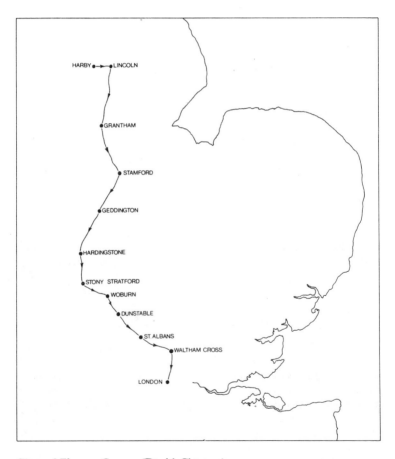

Sites of Eleanor Crosses (David Cheepen)

Penshurst Place

The manor house at the core of Penshurst Place was built (from 1340) by Sir John Pulteney, four times Lord Mayor of London. Apart from the screen (16c), the medieval **Great Hall** is remarkably unchanged, its central hearth not replaced by a fireplace in the wall.

Penshurst Place, which has belonged to the Sidneys since 1552, was the birthplace of Sir Philip Sidney, poet and courtier, in 1554.

Eleanor Crosses

Edward I (reigned 1272–1307), known as 'Longshanks', one of the toughest and tallest (6′ 2″) of English kings, hammered Simon de Montfort and the barons (at the battle of Evesham, 1265) and later the Welsh and Scots.

Eleanor of Castile was the strong woman at his side. He was undoubtedly fond of her – as we have seen, he gave her Leeds Castle. When she died in 1290, he brought her body in stages – twelve in all – from Harby (Lincs) to Westminster. At each resting stage he erected a cross. Three survive – at **Geddington, Hardingstone** (just south of Northampton) and **Waltham Cross**.

The Clergy House Alfriston

The attractive Sussex village of Alfriston, nestling between two shoulders of the Downs, has a number of half-timbered houses. This 14th-century parsonage, the first property acquired by the National Trust (1896), is among them.

The Wool Churches

By the mid-14th century, cloth, superseding wool, was England's chief export. The centres of growing cloth manufacture were Yorkshire, East Anglia and the Cotswolds. The clothiers purchased large quantities of wool, delivered it to the weavers to weave, to the fullers to full, and to the shearmen to finish, eventually receiving it back to sell. Because they paid out wages and accumulated large profits, some have suggested that the clothiers were England's first capitalists.

One of the great clothiers was Thomas Paycocke* of Coggeshall,

Lavenham Church (Guildhall Library)

Essex, in the East Anglian cloth-making district. Coggeshall ranked, as an important centre, after only Norwich, Colchester and Sudbury.

The Paycockes' house (built by Thomas's father) may still be seen. Spot their **Merchant Mark** – an ermine tail like a two-stemmed clover leaf – displayed both inside and outside the house. Branching out from the band of carving running along the house front are all kinds of devices, including a crowned king and queen lying hand in hand.

The moneyed clothiers had a prudential interest in Eternity, purchasing the safety of their souls by rebuilding churches with their wealth. The great perpendicular wool churches are their memorial. The church at Coggeshall is an example. It was probably a Paycocke who built the **Chantry**, where his soul would be prayed for.

A fine wool church – positively cathedral-like – is at **Long Melford**. Its light spaciousness lifts the spirits. Don't hurry! Find time to contemplate.

Particularities: (i) the **window with the Lily-Crucifix** (the lily being the Virgin Mary's traditional flower), (ii) the window said

See Medieval People Eileen Power (Methuen)

Wells Cathedral (West Front) (Guildhall Library)

to have inspired Tenniel, illustrator of 'Alice' and (iii) the 14th-century **alabaster bas-relief** of the Adoration of the Magi.

Approached from Long Melford, the tall tower of the church at Lavenham can be seen from afar, dominating the expanse of fields. Another of the fine wool churches, this one is indebted to the benefactions of clothier Thomas Spring. Be sure to examine the beautifully carved **misericords** on the stalls.

111

The town affords many reminders of past prosperity, the array of timber-framed houses dating from the period when wool, like oil today, was a passport to riches, and those who owned it were as rich as sheikhs. They include the **Old Wool Hall** (c.1500) now incorporated by the Swan Hotel, and the **Guildhall** (1529).

More Cathedrals – Wells, Lincoln, Exeter, York Minster, Bath

Wells

The unrivalled 13c west front was designed as a screen for the display of statuary. The towers were built considerably later.

Inside, the dominating **strainer** (inverted) **arches** of the central crossing – triumphantly ingenious, if incongruous – were constructed (1338–40) because the Early English foundations weren't strong enough to support the (later) central tower. Around this time the **Chapter House** was gloriously revamped into an octagonal building with exuberant **rib vaulting** and **geometrical tracery**.

Don't miss the **fruit stealers** or the jousting knights of the **astronomical clock** (c.1392).

Lincoln

'Si monumentum requiris, circumspice' could have been applied to Hugh of Lincoln, another of the great builder churchmen of the Middle Ages, described by the acerbic Matthew Paris as a 'Persecutor of monks and hammer of all canons and religions'. After an earthquake ruined all but the western facade of the Norman cathedral, it was under Bishop Hugh that reconstruction (in the Early English style) began in 1192. He worked towards the west front from the eastern end, building five chapels behind the high altar. Eventually, in the wake of Hugh's canonisation, the chapels made way for the decorated **Angel Choir** (completed 1280) – fitting accommodation, in its ornate splendour, for the sainted Hugh's earthly remains.

Don't miss (i) the **Bishop's Eye** (ii) the **Dean's Eye** and (iii) the **angels** in the Angel Choir.

Lincoln Cathedral. All but the west end was rebuilt after the earthquake of 1185. Here the Norman work may still be seen. After the Boston Stump, the central tower was the highest in England. (Chris Mountford)

113

Exeter

In the **Nave** 'an avenue of stately trees' awaits your gaze – this is one of the finest vaults in England, a superb example of Decorated Gothic. Don't miss the **Minstrels Gallery** – or, though he's hard to find, the **Exeter Elephant!**

York Minster

Not unusually, the second largest English cathedral grew over a long period of time and incorporates different styles: Early English (transepts), decorated (nave and chapter house), early and late perpendicular (choir and towers).

The Minster's crowning glory (like Canterbury's) is its stained glass. Don't miss (i) the great **East Window**, the largest sheet of medieval glazing in England – it took John Thornton of Coventry three years to complete (for which he was paid £56), (ii) the **Five Sisters Window** (13c. grisaille).

York Minster – after St. Paul's, the largest of English cathedrals. (Chris Mountford)

East Window, York Minster. This is the largest expanse of medieval glazing in England. (Chris Mountford)

115

The Five Sisters Window, York Minster (Chris Mountford)

The 15th cent. Choir Screen, York Minster. It displays statues of English kings from William I to Henry VI. (William I to John here) (Chris Mountford)

117

Bath Abbey

Built in the perpendicular style, 'the lantern of the West' is so called because of its many windows. The glass is mainly modern. Originally confined to the choir, the **fan-tracery** (a purely decorative feature associated with the perpendicular period) was extended over the nave by Sir Gilbert Scott, the great Victorian restorer and champion of neo-Gothic.

Walsingham

Because Walsingham Priory owned the shrine of 'Our Lady of Walsingham', it was a leading centre of medieval pilgrimage. Sitting prettily on this sacred goldmine, the Priory grew rich, and also corrupt, becoming 'one of the least disciplined houses in England' (*The English Reformation* A.G. Dickens). In the 16th century the money-spinning shrine was visited (and scorned) by Erasmus, humanist and friend of Sir Thomas More. Another pilgrim was Henry VIII, who later dissolved all the monasteries, including Walsingham Priory. The shrine, an imagined replica of the Holy House in Nazareth, went too. In 1931 it was reconstructed a short distance from the medieval site, and later, to provide a covering, the present pilgrimage church was added.

Lollardy in Amersham (Bucks)

Many of the key doctrines of the Reformation were anticipated by John Wycliffe, the founder of Lollardy. In the Tudor period Bishop Tunstall would describe Lutheranism as 'foster-daughter of Wycliffe's'. Avoiding the stake, this Oxford philosopher – described as 'the flower of Oxford' – and arch-heretic ended his days in the rectory at Lutterworth, not far from Leicester.

By the year of his death (1384) the movement that started with a single cell at Oxford was spreading far and wide. Amersham was the focal point of a network of underground cells in the Chilterns. A Lollard burned at Smithfield in 1518 confessed that at Windsor he had discovered a Lollard group formed by fugitives from persecution at Amersham, 'a godly and a great company, which had continued in that doctrine and teaching 23 years'.

Henry VI's Foundations

The example of William of Wykeham at Winchester led Henry VI to found the King's College of Our Lady of Eton beside Windsor, intended for 70 poor scholars. Others, called the 'oppidans' – those living in the town – were allowed to attend the lessons. Today there are still scholars and 'oppidans' at Eton.

King's College Cambridge (Guildhall Library)

119

Henry VI's (perpendicular) Chapel is on the south side of the school yard. The 20c fan-vaulting replaced a wooden roof. The founder had intended a stone-vault, but the reverses of his reign had dictated otherwise. Indeed chapel and colleges were lucky to survive at all. Don't overlook (i) the remarkable 15th-century **wall paintings** and (ii) the **fan-vault** of **Lupton's Chapel** (1515).

School Yard has a **statue of King Henry VI** in the centre. **Lower School**, in the brick building (1443) on the north side, is probably the world's oldest classroom in active use.

Henry saw Eton as a feeder for King's College (1446), his other foundation, whose early existence was chequered. Money ran out following the start of the Wars of the Roses, building not being resumed till 1476, by which time the Founder had been despatched. The marvellous **fan vault**, the largest in England, was later ordered by Henry VII. Its weight is transferred to eleven great buttresses on either side and to the corner towers. Henry VII himself didn't live to see the vault's completion in July 1515, sixty-nine years and four days after Henry VI had laid the foundation stone. Most of the stained glass dates from the first half of the 16th century.

8 Place Names*

'Yes. I remember Adlestrop – the name.' Edward Thomas

The antiquity of English place-names may help to explain their perennial fascination. Very few are of recent origin. Camberley (Surrey) dates from 1877. In our century, Peterlee (Co. Durham) – after a miner's leader – and Peacehaven (Sussex) are lonely examples. The majority existed before 1066. Norwegian elements are common in the north-west (e.g. 'thwaite' – clearing). Danish elements are found mainly to the east of Watling Street (A5), approximately the boundary of Danelaw.

A sample:

ADLESTROP (Glos)	OE 'Throp' (village). A personal name provides the 1st element.
ALTHORP (Northants)	OE 'Throp' Olla's village. (Many placenames ending 'Thorp(e)' are pronounced '-throp')
BANBURY (Oxon)	OE 'Bury' (fortified place). A personal name provides the 1st element. The original Banbury Cross was destroyed by Puritans in 1602.
BEDFORD (Beds)	'Beda's Ford'. John Bunyan spent 12 years in the town gaol.
BIRMINGHAM (Warwks)	OE 'Ham'. 'Village of the people of Beorma.'
BRIGHTON (Sussex)	OE 'Tun'. The personal name (Beorhthelm) that provides the 1st element is camouflaged by this 19c shortening of Brighthelmstone. The favourite resort of the Prince Regent, builder of the Royal Pavilion.
BRISTOL (Avon)	OE 'Brycg stowe' (Holy place by the Bridge). The perpendicular St. Mary Redcliffe was described by Queen Elizabeth I as 'the fairest, the goodliest, and most famous parish church

*See *The Concise Oxford Dictionary of English Place Names* E. Ekwall.

in England'. In 1497 the Cabots sailed from here. In the 18th century the wealth of the thriving seaport was boosted by the African slave trade. Brunel's 'Great Western' was launched here in 1838.

BUCKINGHAM (Bucks)   OE 'Hamm' (c.f. 'Ham') – Land in a river bend'. This land (in a bend of the Great Ouse) was occupied by Bucca's people.

CAMBRIDGE (Cambs)   OE 'Grantebrycg'. The river name 'Cam' was later substituted for 'Granta' (also a river name).

GLOUCESTER (Glos)   'Cester' (Fort) is preceded by the contraction of a Romanised Celtic root ('Glevum' – Bright Place). The cathedral (Norman nave, perpendicular choir and transepts) contains the tomb of Edward II.

GRANTCHESTER (Cambs)   In this case the 'chester' element is from an OE word for 'settlers'. 'Stands the Church clock at ten to three? And is there honey still for tea?'. The clock immortalised by Rupert Brooke has stood the test of time.

HENLEY (Oxon)   OE 'ley' – a high clearing.

HUISH EPISCOPI (Som)   Norman 'Huish' – a measure of land. This land belonged to the Bishop of Bath and Wells.

LINCOLN (Lincs)   Celtic 'Lindon' (pool) was Latinised to 'Lindum', with 'Colonia' (a settlement of retired soldiers) placed after. The modern name combines both elements.

MALVERN (Worcs)   From the Celtic for 'Bare hill'.

NOTTINGHAM (Notts)   'Village of Snot's people'. Because the Normans found difficulty with 's's' when followed by another consonant, inelegant 'Snotingaham' arrived at 'Nottingham'. Outside the (mainly 17c) castle, modern statues of Robin Hood and his Merrie Men help to preserve an imaginary link. The Robin Hood legend dates from the late 14th century.

OXFORD (Oxon)   'A ford for oxen'.

PETERBOROUGH (Cambs)   A 14th-century replacement name for OE Medeshamstede – 'Meda's homestead'. '(Saint) Peter's chartered town'. The Norman cathedral is dedicated to St. Peter.

RICKMANSWORTH (Herts)	OE 'Worth' (enclosure) is combined with a personal name. At different times William Penn and George Eliot lived here.
SALISBURY (Wilts)	Romano-British 'Sorbiodunum'. OE 'Bury' was substituted for '-dunum'. The Norman form of the name was 'Salesbiri'.
STOKE POGES (Bucks)	OE 'stoke' (Daughter settlement). The land was held in the 13th century by Hubert le Pugeis. In the churchyard Gray heard the curfew toll the knell of parting day.
STONETHWAITE (Cumb)	The Scandinavian suffix (clearing) is common in the Lake District.
TREMAINE (Cornwall)	Celtic 'Tre-' (Farm, Village) is common in Cornwall.
WARWICK (Warwks)	OE 'Wic'. 'Dwellings near weir'. The fine (mainly 14th c) castle overlooks the Avon.
WHITCHURCH CANONICORUM (Som)	The 'white (stone) church' belonged to a Norman abbey. A pre-Reformation shrine to St. Candida has been preserved. One of Somerset's many place-name gems.
WINCHESTER (Hants)	The 1st element, combined with 'chester', is from the Romano-British Venta Belgarum. The cathedral is the longest in England.

9. England Under the Tudors and Stuarts

At the Public Record Office it is is possible to see a book of receipts, issued by the Treasurer of the King's Chamber, with each entry subscribed 'H'. By his personal grasp of government, in particular royal finance, Henry VII helped to make possible the longevity of the dynasty. Pious as well as businesslike, Henry's autographed prayer book is at Chatsworth House.

At first, success was far from guaranteed. Outside Newark, on the south side of the Trent, lies the village of East Stoke, where on 16 June 1487 Yorkist rebels were intercepted and defeated by Henry, as they moved towards London. The rebellion was in the name of a ten year old called Lambert Simnel, posing as the Earl of Warwick, the last male Yorkist with a direct claim to the throne. Henry gave thanks for his victory amidst the gothic splendours of Lincoln Cathedral. Simnel ended up in the royal kitchen, and the real Warwick was executed. In 1497 the Yorkists were crushed again. This time they rebelled in the name of the youthful Perkin Warbeck, impersonating Richard Duke of York, the younger of the two murdered princes. Warbeck sought sanctuary in Beaulieu Abbey (Hants) but he didn't elude Henry's grasp.

At the head of the Grand Staircase in Windsor Castle stands the last surviving armour of the more remembered Henry VIII, a suit for a grossly corpulent frame. By this time Henry had gone to seed. It's the ageing, seedy Henry that dominates the popular imagination. In the early years of his rule, he had a fine, knightly physique together with the intellectual accomplishments of a model Renaissance prince. Owing to Henry VII, he inherited a strong administration and a full treasury. The nobility, weakened by the Wars of the Roses, was suffering from a battery of attainders and executions – Henry VIII would continue where his father left off. No longer would they overawe the Monarch. Significantly, in 1450 the richest peer had been the Duke of York worth £3500, about 1/10th of the Crown's income. By 1559 the richest was the Duke of Norfolk with roughly £6000, by which time the Crown was twenty-six times as wealthy.

However, there were others, starting on a lower rung in the social scale, who did very well, in some cases by making themselves conspicuously useful to the Tudors. 'Take but degree away, Untune that string, and hark what discord follows!' wrote Shakespeare. This could be called the official view, though the string was being constantly untuned – by, among others, the Bard of Avon! Let us take some well-known examples.

John Spencer, a Warwickshire squire, was charged by Thomas Wolsey's anti-enclosure commission in 1517 and ordered to pull down hedges and restore lands to tillage (in fairness, the manor he'd purchased was enclosed already). The Spencers came by more land elsewhere and established themselves at Althorp, where they founded – not one but two – noble families: the Earls Spencer of Althorp and the Spencer-Churchills, dukes of Marlborough. A new aristocracy was being steadily forged.

Some came from nowhere and rose rapidly to dizzy heights in the service of the Tudor state. John Morton climbed through the ranks till, in the reign of Henry VII, he ended up with both a cardinal's hat and the Lord Chancellor's seal. He is credited with the invention of a Catch 22 device – and one still useful to Inspectors of Taxes! A magnate living in style was obviously able to pay high taxes. The other prong of 'Morton's fork' pierced the nobleman who lived modestly – he must be stashing his wealth. Morton himself favoured ostentation. As Bishop of Ely (and therefore owning the manor of Hatfield) he built Old Hatfield Palace, whose magnificent banqueting hall still stands in the west gardens of Hatfield House.

Morton's career set a pattern for the still more spectacular advance of Thomas Wolsey, son of an Ipswich cattle-dealer. Like Morton, Wolsey was a member of an Oxford college. When bursar at Magdalen, he may have designed the perpendicular Magdalen Tower, one of Oxford's great landmarks. When a cardinal, and Henry VIII's Lord Chancellor, he founded Cardinal College (renamed Christ Church long after his fall).

Both Wolsey and his royal master loved flaunting their wealth and power. Enriched by his revenues as Archbishop of York, Bishop of Durham and Abbot of St. Albans, Wolsey outdid the King with Hampton Court. In 1538 Henry flattened the Surrey village of Ewell to build the thickly turreted Nonesuch Palace, later demolished by a mistress of Charles II.

Wolsey fell from grace in 1529 because a Prince of the Church could hardly defy the Pope on the King's behalf when Henry sought to rid himself of Catherine of Aragon. Henry needed a male heir, and his religious scruples about being married to his brother's widow were probably genuine, but the most pressing explanation of his state of mind at this time must be sought at moated, 13th-century Hever Castle, the Kentish home of the Boleyn family. In this idyllic spot Henry may well have met Anne for the first time – her elder sister had already passed through his bed. The writing was now on the wall for Tudor England's most celebrated 'New Man'. Families like the Spencers would stand by and applaud. Most conveniently for him, Wolsey died at Leicester Abbey on the way south to face charges. Another parvenu, Thomas Cromwell, was waiting in the wings to take over. Cromwell, careful – until near the end – to move with the grain of the royal will, which he probably helped to mould, master-minded the divorce (carried through in Thomas Cranmer's archiepiscopal court at Dunstable), then the necessary break with Rome, and the subsequent royal grab of the vast monastic lands. Henry's sale of these lands for financial windfalls to subsidise the Sport of Kings both consolidated the position of established landed families, and allowed others to join the landed elite.

One beneficiary was Nicholas Bacon, father of Francis. The son of the sheepreeve to the Abbey of Bury St. Edmunds was well placed to take advantage of Henry VIII's prodigality, becoming owner of many of the farms his father had helped to manage. From here Nicholas Bacon spread his wings. At Gorhambury, just outside St. Albans, lie the ruins of his great house, which Francis inherited. It was partly built with the stone of the dissolved abbey.

Nicholas Bacon was a key servant of Elizabeth I, Henry's daughter by Anne Boleyn. Another was William Cecil. By the time of Elizabeth's accession, having survived Mary's 'holy bonfires', perhaps because, in a contemporary phrase, he was 'sprung from willow', he had already started to build Burghley House (Lincs), to be finally completed in the late 1580's. It was a long process because Cecil had another project on his plate. This was Theobalds (Herts), which became the largest house in England, with fine courtyards extending over $\frac{1}{4}$ mile. Like the almost equally huge Holdenby (Holmby) House in Northants, built by Sir Christopher Hatton, another of Elizabeth's councillors, it hasn't passed the test of time. Sir Christopher, the Queen's dancing master extraordinary, bought nearby Kirby Hall (which still stands) as well as building Holdenby Hall. Financial ruin was the result. In this respect he was less fortunate than Sir Francis Willoughby, who built Wollaton Hall (Notts) on the proceeds of iron and coal – the very model of an upwardly mobile Tudor gentleman, eager to seize all the opportunities. The Queen's master mason, Robert Smythson, who worked at Wollaton, also designed Sir John Thynne's Longleat (Wilts) with its

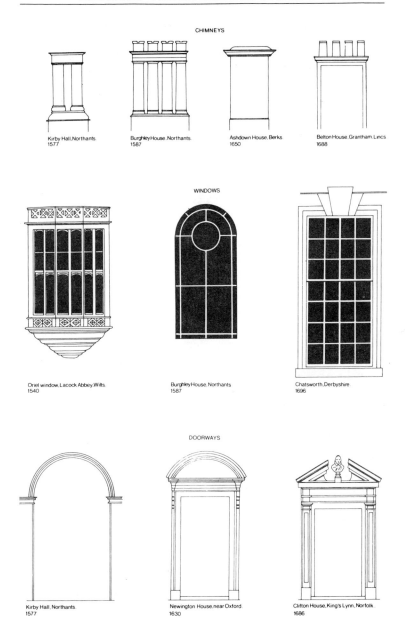

CHIMNEYS

Kirby Hall, Northants.
1577

Burghley House, Northants.
1587

Ashdown House, Berks.
1650

Belton House, Grantham, Lincs
1688

WINDOWS

Oriel window, Lacock Abbey, Wilts.
1540

Burghley House, Northants
1587

Chatsworth, Derbyshire.
1696

DOORWAYS

Kirby Hall, Northants.
1577

Newington House, near Oxford.
1630

Clifton House, King's Lynn, Norfolk.
1686

Tudor and Stuart chimneys, windows and doorways (David Cheepen)

glittering array of glass and bay windows – a sort of Tudor Crystal Palace! – as well as Hardwick Hall, on behalf of Bess of Hardwick, Countess of Shrewsbury, whose formidable qualities rivalled those of the Queen herself.

Needless to say, a woman *had* to be formidable if she was to prosper in the male-dominated 16th-century world – and even then, like Mary Queen of Scots, she could come unstuck. Elizabeth possessed the intellectual accomplishments of her father, and far more common sense. Never irrationally cruel, she was extremely tough when the occasion demanded. She could also use or invoke her supposedly gentler sex to command loyalty and affection.

Elizabeth's toughness was fostered by the experiences of childhood, much of which was spent at Old Hatfield Palace, expropriated by Henry VIII from the Bishops of Ely as a nursery for his children. While Anne Boleyn was in favour, Elizabeth's position was totally secure. Catholic Mary, Catherine of Aragon's daughter, was even ordered to wait on her. Despite this humiliation, the principled Mary remained steadfastly loyal to her mother, who died at Kimbolton Castle (Cambs) in 1536.

Elizabeth's childhood security was rudely shattered by the execution of her mother. Later on, when Mary became Queen, even Elizabeth's life was endangered. Under house arrest at Hatfield, it is said that the news of Mary's death reached her as she sat under an oak tree in the grounds. Her first Council of State was held in the Palace.

Of course, Elizabeth's accession didn't remove all danger. Roman Catholics were bound to object to a Protestant Queen, albeit one who didn't wish 'to carve windows into men's souls'. In 1567 the Catholic Earls of Northumberland (Percy) and Westmorland (Neville) rose against her. The rebellion fizzled out, and the earls went to the block. Raby Castle (Neville) and Alnwick Castle (Percy) would stand, or crumble, as memorials to the era of the overmighty magnate. With Catholic Mary Queen of Scots in the wings until 1587, there were more hairbrained Catholic schemes but no serious or widespread disaffection.

It wasn't to reassert royal authority that Elizabeth made her progresses, but simply to be seen – and to give courtiers the chance (taken, in spite of expense, with alacrity!) to entertain her lavishly. 'God send us both long to enjoy her for whom we both mean to exceed our purses. . . .' wrote Cecil, fresh from extending Theobalds, to Hatton, who had just built Holdenby Hall. With her streak of parsimony, Elizabeth (unlike her father) didn't build palaces herself, but encouraged others to do so. On her annual summer progress she reaped the benefit. This was when the whole household took to the dusty highways, with hundreds of carts carrying the baggage, that included furnishings for bare and draughty rooms.* Elizabeth herself rode on horseback or in an open litter – the object was to be seen. Ten or twelve miles were covered each day – quite enough given all those carts! In theory, the hosts en route merely surrendered their houses, all costs being borne by the Household. In practice, they vied with each other to provide the most extravagant hospitality. In 1575 the Earl of Leicester spared no expense at Kenilworth for three memorable weeks. Two years later Sir Nicholas Bacon footed a bill of £577 after a four day visit by Queen and Court to Gorhambury.

Elizabeth didn't want the fun to come to an end. In the twilight of her reign, when courtiers were heard to complain at the prospect of another progress, the Queen (aged 66) told the old to stay behind. Her spirit was indomitable, and she couldn't bear the thought of death – even talk of the succession was taboo. Her moods grew variable, though she still could charm the birds off the trees! 'When she smiled,' wrote Sir John Harington, her godson, at this time, 'it was a pure sunshine that everyone did choose to bask in if they could; but anon came a storm from a sudden gathering of clouds, and the thunder fell in wondrous manner on all alike.'

Behind the scenes, Robert Cecil, Burghley's misshapen son, arranged the accession of James I, a fun-loving Scot with a taste for polemics. This move had Elizabeth's deathbed approval. Cecil became the most powerful minister of the grateful king. As the channel through which royal patronage flowed, he exercised huge influence. England became known as Regnum Cecilianum. While the king hunted, or pamphleteered, or fussed over his current favourite, his Lord Treasurer conducted the daily business of government, as his father had done for Gloriana. His finest hour was the unmasking of the Gunpowder Plot. Some have suggested that Cecil, being determined to blacken the Catholics by any means, was behind the Plot, though the existence of a 'Cecilgate' has yet to be proved.

James persuaded his invaluable minister to exchange the manor of Theobalds for that of Hatfield. Cecil proceeded (1607–11) to build Hatfield House which, unlike Theobalds, has stood the test of time. He died in 1612, by when Regnum Cecilianum was already on the wane.

At some stage Englishmen embarked on the high road to Civil War. Historians cannot agree when – or why – that was, or whether there was a high road at all! James made outrageous remarks, such as comparing Kings to gods. His entourage looked decadent to sober

*see Sir John Neale's *Elizabeth I* (Penguin)

Puritans – indeed it was. Yet no Civil War between King and Parliament could have been predicted in the year of his death (1625).

James's stammering younger son was both duplicitous and perversely prone to miscalculation – he may even have nursed a death-wish. There was an attractive side to Charles – his love of fine art and architecture. He put Inigo Jones to work on the Earl of Pembroke's Wilton House (Wilts), the house which, according to John Aubrey, he loved 'above all other places'. His devotion to the Anglican Church led him into trouble when, with Archbishop Laud, he tried to foist his Arminian (Anglo-Catholic) interpretation of Anglicanism upon everybody else, including Puritans and Scots. Unusually for an English king, Charles was loyal to his wife, French-born Henrietta Maria. This too led him into trouble when, in January 1542, partly because he feared for her safety, he attempted to arrest leading members of the parliamentary opposition. This action seemed to confirm what parliamentary propaganda had long been saying – Charles was trying to establish an absolutism. What mattered was not the objective facts, but how people with axes to grind chose to interpret what they saw. The result of the crisis with Parliament was that Charles, rather unwisely, quit London and prepared for war, much of which he would spend trying to get his capital back.

Above the early Tudor mansion of Compton Wynyates (Warwicks), once visited by Henry VIII, rises the Edge Hill escarpment, where, on 23rd October 1642, the first (and indecisive) engagement of the Civil War was fought. A small monument nearby is to Sir Edward Verney, the King's Standard bearer, who was killed. The Verneys, whose home was Claydon House (Bucks), illustrate how the Civil War even divided families – Sir Edmund's son was a parliamentarian. Landed gentry families like the Verneys played the leading roles in the war, while the nobility, the leading players in the Wars of the Roses, now helped, or hindered, the gentry. The Earl of Manchester, for example, was more of a hindrance to Oliver Cromwell, who had him removed from his command.

Cromwell's Ironsides, convinced that theirs was a Godly cause, sang hymns before going into battle. In terms of military tactics they were far superior to Prince Rupert's royalist cavalry. As the Earl of Clarendon would explain, 'Though the King's troops prevailed in the charge and routed those they charged, they never rallied themselves again in order, nor could be brought to make a second charge again the same day ... whereas Cromwell's troops, if they prevailed, or thought they were beaten and presently routed, rallied again and stood in good order till they received new orders.'

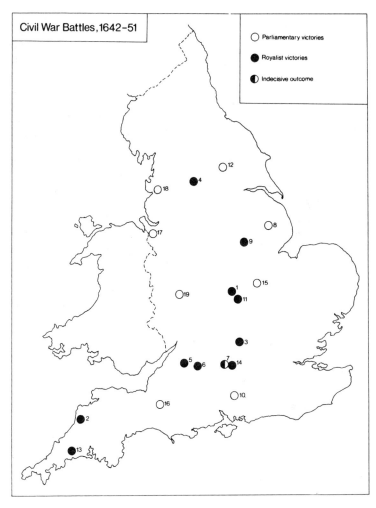

Civil War Battles, 1642–51

○ Parliamentary victories

● Royalist victories

◑ Indecisive outcome

1. Edgehill, 1642
2. Stratton, 1643
3. Chalgrove Field, 1643
4. Adwalton Moor, 1643
5. Lansdown, 1643
6. Roundway Down, 1643
7. Newbury I, 1643
8. Winceby, 1643
9. Newark, 1644
10. Cheriton, 1644
11. Cropredy Bridge, 1644
12. Marston Moor, 1644
13. Lostwithiel, 1644
14. Newbury II, 1644
15. Naseby, 1645
16. Langport, 1645
17. Rowton Heath, 1645
18. Preston, 1648
19. Worcester, 1651

Map showing the main battles 1642–51 (David Cheepen)

131

The turning point of the war came on 2nd July 1644, when the armies clashed on Marston Moor, between York and Wetherby. The Ironsides, magnificently drilled by Cromwell, took Rupert's cavalry by surprise. Re-entering the fray later on, they demolished the royalist centre. The victory was conclusive, and the king lost York and the north.

The village of Naseby lies between Northampton and Market Harborough. Near here, in June 1645, the King himself was defeated, and mainly owing to the Ironsides. The battlefield has changed little since 1645. A monument on the ridge marks the place where the Roundheads took up their position.

The writing was on the wall for the royalists, though Charles

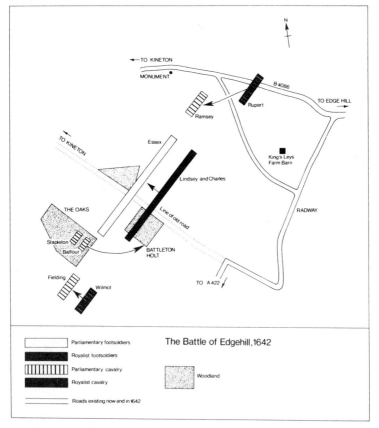

Plan of the Battle of Edgehill (1642) (David Cheepen)

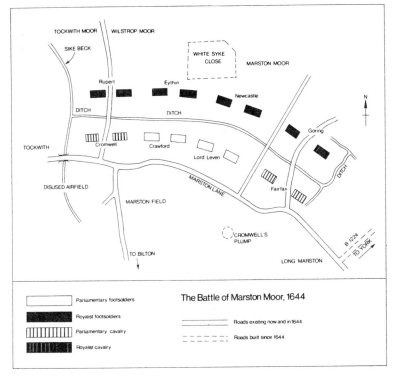

Plan of the Battle of Marston Moor (1644) (David Cheepen)

fought on till May 1646. Later he was kept by Parliament at Holdenby House, not far from the battlefield of Naseby. Eventually he escaped from Newmarket, where he was being held by the army, to the Isle of Wight. At Carisbrooke Castle, where he briefly resided, one may see a Book of Common Prayer, signed by the King, and the nightcap worn by him on the night before his execution, in January 1647.

At Tunbridge Wells in Kent, the plain brick church of King Charles the Martyr is a reminder of the cult that grew up after his execution. Royalist sentiment would help to restore Charles II in 1660 but in 1651 this seemed a distant prospect. Boscobel House (Salop) is a small 17th-century manor house, where the future Charles II took refuge following his disastrous defeat by Cromwell at Worcester. In those days it was surrounded by dense woods. Charles spent some of his time in an oak tree. From an acorn of this original tree the existing 'royal oak' grew. Charles moved on to Moseley Old Hall (also standing today) where he stayed three nights, part of the time in

133

a priest hole. Altogether he spent forty-three days on the run, spiriting himself from hideout to hideout until he reached Shoreham on the Sussex coast, where he boarded a fishing-smack for France. Nine years later, with Oliver dead and his army despised, Charles was welcomed back. However, support was conditional upon 'good behaviour'. Charles complied because he had no wish to 'go on his travels again'.

Brixham is an attractive fishing port on the South Devon coast. On 5th November 1688 William of Orange was brought here by the so-called Protestant wind. The stone on which he stepped from his boat has been preserved. At Hardwick Hall (Derbys) the 'Revolution Chair' is said to have been used by the fourth Earl of Devonshire when planning the invitation to William, who was James II's son-in-law.

James II, Charles II's younger brother and successor in 1685, had failed to keep his side of the Restoration bargain. By championing Rome he trod on the corns of the (Anglican) landed establishment, which he aimed to thwart by an unlikely alliance with the Dissenters. In the grounds of the 17th-century meeting house at Jordans (Bucks) are buried Quaker William Penn, his two wives and countless progeny. For a brief period Penn found he was the King's chief ally. In the end the Dissenters refused to be convinced. Penn was merely discredited, but the King lost his throne. Decisively, the landowning class had come to fear for both its religion and property. The last straw was the birth of the King's son in June 1688.

William had an easy ride. James was no match, especially after the desertion of John Churchill, the future Duke of Marlborough. James's flight wasn't quite the end of the Stuarts, for Mary, his daughter, ruled with William until her death in 1694. Anne, another daughter, ascended the throne on William's death in 1702.

The Glorious Revolution of 1688–9 signalled the advent of limited, or constitutional, monarchy. Its framework was the Bill of Rights, the Revolutionary Settlement. When the first Hanoverian arrived in 1714, after none of Anne's seventeen children had survived, he came to reign, rather than to rule. As George I hated England, and knew no English, this arrangement suited him perfectly.

Poet, antiquarian and the first of the itinerant diarists of Tudor and Stuart times, John Leland travelled through England in the 1530s. His official task was to salvage the manuscripts of dissolved monasteries. Near the end of this period, Celia Fiennes journeyed tirelessly. Some of her experiences were set down in 'Through

England on a Side Saddle in the time of William and Mary'.

The England known to Celia Fiennes wasn't totally different from John Leland's. Cloth making was still the most significant English industry. 'It turns the most money in a weeke,' Celia said, 'of anything in England.' She described how the wool was farmed out to workers in their cottages by capitalist clothiers or middlemen – as it had been in Paycocke's time.

Apart from cloth-making, Celia was a keen observer of industry, especially mining, in which there was a family financial interest. In Cornwall 'I went a mile farther on the hills and soe came where they were digging in the Tinn mines, there was at least twenty mines all in sight which employs a great many people at work, almost night and day, but constantly all and every day including the Lords day which they are forced to, to prevent their mines being overflowed with water....'

Though the level of English industry didn't increase dramatically between the 1530s and 1690s, there was a marked growth of population and towns. In the 1530s most towns were relatively uncrowded. For example, Norwich was 'either a City in an Orchard or an Orchard in a City; so equally are Houses and Trees blended in it'.* By 1700 congestion within decayed walls and a surburban sprawl without were far commoner. Bristol had overtaken Norwich as the second largest city after London. Like Liverpool, it prospered from the transatlantic slave trade. Celia Fiennes was greatly impressed. She saw 'the harbour was full of ships carrying coales and all sorts of commodityes to other parts....' Leeds she portrayed as 'very rich and very proud; they have provision soe plentifull that they may live with very little expense had and get much variety'.

When Sir Thomas More famously remarked that sheep were devouring men, he was referring to the effect of enclosures for profitable sheep-farming. As a consequence the open fields of medieval times started to disappear, the strips being consolidated into compact, hedged fields. Both Leland and Celia Fiennes lived before the great age of enclosure, when the face of England's countryside was radically altered for good.

The victims of Tudor enclosure would naturally have agreed with Sir Thomas More. Often taking to the roads, they helped to create the problem of vagabondage, so perplexing to the Tudor bureaucrats, who framed the Poor Law as an instrument of social control. The genesis of Oliver Twist's workhouse was the parochial house of correction of Elizabethan times.

The Making of The English Landscape

Meanwhile, gentry and yeomen built, or extended, houses of a very different kind. Many, like Little Moreton Hall in Cheshire, continued to be timbered, but brick and stone was increasingly the fashion for the better-off. In 1577 William Harrison, a travelling parson, noted that chimneys had become general. This was due to the increased use of coal, as well as to the increased use of brick. By 1700 there were many bigger, and more solid, houses than in the 1530s. The home of the better-off Englishman had already become his castle.

Further Reading

Peace, Print and Protestantism 1450–1558 C.S.L. Davies (Paladin, 1977)

The English Reformation A.G. Dickens (Fontana, 1964)

Tudor England S.T. Bindoff (Penguin, 1969)

Queen Elizabeth I J.E. Neale (Cape, 1934, Pelican Biography (Penguin 1971)

Elizabeth I and the Unity of England J. Hurstfield (Penguin, 1971)

English Society 1580–1680 Keith Wrightson (Hutchinson, 1982)

The History of Myddle Richard Gough Ed: David Hey (Penguin, 1981)

The Stuarts J.P. Kenyon (Fontana, 1966)

God's Englishman Christopher Hill (Penguin, 1970)

Reappraisals in History J.H. Hexter (Longman, 2nd edition 1967)

The Glorious Revolution of 1688 M. Ashley (Hodder 1966)

England under Queen Anne G.M. Trevelyan (Longman, 3 vols, 1930–4)

10 Historic England (4)

Knole

Thomas Bourchier was Archbishop of Canterbury from 1456 to 86 – the record tenure of the see. He paid £226 1s 4d for this estate, then built the present house. Until 1538 Knole was a home of the arch-bishops, the last of whom was Thomas Cranmer. Prone to jealousy of the fine houses of his leading servants, Henry VIII persuaded him to part with it, and in this way Knole became the property of the Crown. Later it was given by Elizabeth to a cousin, Thomas Sackville, court politician and part-time playwright. As James I's Lord Treasurer, he had the task of raising cash for the hard-pressed Crown. One recourse of his (sure to please the royal author of *The Counterblast against Tobacco* was to increase heftily the tax on tobacco. For loyal service he was made 1st Earl of Dorset. Not till the last five years of his life (he died in 1608) was the Earl at Knole, where he worked hard on the interior, for example building the **Great Staircase** and transforming the **Great Hall** by adding oak panelling, an oak screen and a plasterwork ceiling.

Christ Church Oxford

In 1525 Wolsey, when in his pomp, founded Cardinal College. In 1546 – cardinals no longer being fashionable! – the name was changed to Christ Church. **Tom Tower** over **Wolsey's Gateway** was built by Wren in 1681. 'Great Tom' inside weights $6\frac{1}{4}$ tons (compared to Big Ben's $13\frac{1}{2}$). **Tom Quad** (the largest in Oxford) was built by Wolsey. Spot the stone plinths that were intended to support the columns of the cloister that, owing to his fall, failed to materialise. **The Staircase** (17c) has a fan-tracery roof (last example of the style in England).

On the site of an 8th-century nunnery (founded by St. Frideswide) the College **Chapel** (Oxford Cathedral) goes back to Norman times. In the **Nave** round and octagonal pillars alternate with each other. The soaring vault of the **Choir** (c.1500) contrasts with their romanesque solidity.

Don't overlook the **Watching Chamber** of St. Frideswide, or the fine **tombs**, such as lady Furnival's.

The Bodleian and the Martyrs

Founded by Sir Thomas Bodley in 1602, the origin of the Bodleian was the collection of Humphrey, Duke of Gloucester (1391–1447), the popular and astute brother of Henry V. This was briefly housed in a specially built **Library** (which may be seen) above the magnificently fan-vaulted **Divinity School**, where Cranmer, Ridley and Latimer were interrogated in 1555 – all three would pay dearly for their Protestant beliefs. A **cross** in **Broad Street** (opposite Balliol College) marks the spot where they were burned at the stake. The **Martyr's Memorial** is in **Magdalen Street**. As the flames licked around, Latimer told the younger Ridley to 'be of good cheer'. Less heroic than Latimer, Cranmer signed a recantation. Once he grasped it wouldn't save him, he publicly disowned it from the pulpit of **St. Mary's Church** – 'And forasmuch as my hand offended, writing contrary to my heart . . . when I come to the fire it shall first be burned.'

The White Horse (Cambridge) and the Reformation

Cambridge was a seed-bed of Lutheranism in England. A passage off King's Parade, nearly opposite the main gate of King's, leads to the small church of **St. Edward, King and Martyr**, whch still contains the **Pulpit** (c.1510) from which first generation Protestants, Barnes, Bilney and Latimer, preached their sermons. Robert Barnes was an Augustinian prior, whose friary stood in St. Edward's parish on the site of the Cavendish Laboratory. The Lutherans would meet regularly at The White Horse, called 'Little Germany', which also lay within the parish. Significantly, most of the early Protestant leaders, including Tyndale and Cranmer, were in Cambridge when the White Horse gatherings were taking place.

Hever Castle

As the childhood home of Anne Boleyn (1507–36), the Tudor association of this late-13th-century moated castle in the Weald of Kent is particularly strong. Here, traditionally, she first met Henry VIII.

Trinity College Cambridge

Henry VIII wasn't to be outdone by Wolsey! In 1546 he established his own college – at Cambridge. The **Great Gateway** of 1518 leads to the **Great Court**. On the north side stands the **Tudor Chapel**; on the south, the **Queen's Gate** with a statue of Elizabeth I; on the west, the **Hall** (1604–5), with the great **Kitchen** south of it. **Nevile's Cloister Court** leads to **Wren's Library** containing bookcases carved by Grinling Gibbons.

Moated Hever Castle (E. S. Kiek)

Trinity College Cambridge (Guildhall Library)

Melford Hall and Kentwell Hall, Long Melford.

Sir William Cordell, a successful Elizabethan lawyer who rose to be Master of the Rolls, built Melford Hall, a multi-turreted house of mellow red brick. There were originally four wings surrounding the courtyard (the gatehouse wing not surviving).

William Clopton, his older contemporary (N.B. the **Clopton Chantry** in the church) built moated Kentwell Hall on an E-plan. The impressive **avenue of limes** was planted in 1678. *Not to be missed*: the authentic recreations of Tudor life mounted in the house and grounds for a fortnight each summer. Write to Patrick and Judith Phillips at Kentwell Hall for details (school parties welcome).

Burghley House

Perhaps the greatest achievement of medieval Englishmen was their cathedrals. The Tudors, who concentrated on secular architecture, built stately homes instead. With their courtyards, towers and crenellations, they showed the influence of the medieval castle. From Italy the classical, or Renaissance, style also made itself felt. This was seen

Burghley House (English Tourist Board)

early on at **Layer Marney Hall** (Essex) built by the captain of Henry VIII's bodyguard, with its totally symmetrical gatehouse towers. In a spirit of compromise – both in religion and in architecture Elizabethans favoured the *via media* – classical symmetry and Gothic irregularity were combined.

Burghley House, built by William Cecil, is an example of the fusion. To Defoe (c.1724) it looked 'more like a town than a house; the towers and the pinnacles so high, and placed at such a distance from one another, look like so many distant parish-churches in a great town ...' The house has three symmetrical fronts, and octagonal corner towers surmounted by turrets. The main gatehouse has four more turreted towers. Burghley's idea was to build lavishly, so that the Queen would wish to stay – and she did, on a number of occasions, at the cost of over £3000 a time.

The Park was landscaped by Capability Brown (c.1760).

Longleat

John Thynne, a beneficiary of the dissolution of the monasteries, acquired the land and priory buildings at Longleat in 1541. He survived near the top in the cut-and-thrust world of Tudor politics, was knighted by Protector Somerset, and grew very rich – so rich that when in 1567 the house he had already built at Longleat burned down he could build another. This is the Lantern House we see today. Symmetrical facades lined with classical statues are combined in this stately home of glistening glass with irregular turrets, some of which were used as 'banqueting rooms' for intimate parties.

The grounds were landscaped in the 18th century by Capability Brown.

Shakespeare and Stratford

John Shakespeare, father of William, arrived in the important market town of Stratford around 1551, prospered, then married well. His wife, Mary Arden, was one of the eight daughters of a comfortable yeoman, whose half-timbered Tudor **farmhouse** is at **Wilmcote,** just west of Stratford, where in a surviving house on the north side of **Henley Street**, William was born on 23 April 1564. The west part of the house is furnished as it might have been in his day, and the east part is a museum.

William attended the Grammar School, housed in the 15th-century **Guildhall**. In 1582 he married a local girl – in a famous biographer's words, 'not without circumstances of irregularity and

Shakespeare's Birthplace (David Cheepen)

haste'* – then left her holding the babies – Susanna and the twins, Hannet and Judith – while he went off to London. **Anne Hathaway's Cottage,** his wife's childhood home, complete with Elizabethan bedstead, is at **Shottery,** one mile west of Stratford.

In 1597, the rich and successful dramatist purchased New Place, the largest house in Stratford. Alderman John would have been delighted. William was a chip off the old block – upwardly mobile to his fingertips!

Shakespeare finally retired to Stratford in 1611, dying here on 23 April 1616. He is buried in the **Chancel** of **Holy Trinity Church.** As for New Place, the fine residence was insensitively demolished by an 18th-century parson, who was consequently driven out of town.

---

*Shakespeare Walter Raleigh (Macmillan)

Hardwick Hall

By the time she was 60, Bess of Hardwick had been widowed four times. The fortune left by her last three husbands enabled her to build a vast, yet compact, mansion – perhaps the finest Elizabethan house, and most likely the work of Robert Smythson. In 1597, at the age of 77, Bess was able to move in.

The great chamber and the long gallery are the important new features of 16th-century houses, the great chamber taking over from the hall as the principal room for feasting as well as for ceremony. At Hardwick both are situated on the second floor. The winding stone **Staircase** was designed to be grand enough for the Queen as she

Hardwick Hall (English Tourist Board)

144

progressed with her courtiers from the hall to the chamber. The **Long Gallery**, running the full length of the house, is the best in England.

Outside, admire the beauty of the **cresting** (**ES** with coronet) on the six symmetrical towers.

Camden's Britannia

'Camden, though time all monuments obscure
Yet thy just labours ever shall endure.'
Edmund Spenser

Intellectual luminary, associate of Spenser and Sidney, William Camden (1551–1623) did for England and Wales that which John Stow, his friend and contemporary, performed for London. Camden's county by county survey first appeared in 1586. For each he described 'the bounds and qualities of soil, the places memorable in antiquity, the dukes, earls, barons, and the most antient and illustrious families; for it is impossible to mention them all'. Indeed, the poor are left out of Britannia.

Camden travelled widely. In 1600, for example, accompanied by Sir Robert Bruce Cotton, he journeyed to Carlisle, surveying the northern counties. He also read a lot, using the libraries of friends such as Cotton (whose collection would help establish the British Museum) and Stow. He was indebted to Leland's Itinerary. Leland (like Celia Fiennes) was mainly interested in the sights he observed, but for Camden, first and foremost an antiquarian, their past – and human – associations were more important. Both Camden and Leland helped to preserve the memory of monuments Time might otherwise have obscured.

Hatfield House

Robert Lyminge designed Hatfield House under the Earl of Salisbury's watchful eye on the E-plan (two wings joined by a central block) in a predominantly Renaissance style. Important features include (i) the **Marble Hall**, with, at one end, the **Minstrels' Gallery**. (ii) the **Long Gallery**, running the entire length of the south front (c.180 feet). (iii) The beautifully carved **Grand Staircase**. Look for the **dual portrait** – the figure in the foreground is the 4th Earl. This earl was an associate of the Duke of Monmouth, and even owned his portrait. When Monmouth rebelled, he prudently super-

Hatfield House (David Cheepen)

imposed his own portrait. However, the duke's head has been fortuitously uncovered.

Though Robert Cecil (the 1st Earl) built Hatfield House, the presiding spirit is undoubtedly Elizabeth I – the **Rainbow Portrait** and the **Ermine Portrait** (Nicholas Hilliard) are in the Marble Hall. Elizabeth only knew Old Hatfield Palace, of which the Banqueting Hall, with its magnificent timbered **roof,** has survived.

Blickling Hall

In an earlier house on this site Anne Boleyn spent her childhood. This one is Jacobean. The similarities – e.g. ogee-capped corner towers – with Hatfield House are not surprising since they were designed by the same man – Robert Lyminge. The gallery (120 feet), with its fine plastered ceiling, contains a library of 12,000 volumes, many printed before 1500.

Wilton House

Dating from Elizabeth's reign, Wilton House (home of the Earls of Pembroke) was a favourite residence of Charles I. 'King Charles I did love Wilton above all other places, and came thither every summer,' noted John Aubrey. 'It was he that did put Philip, Earl of Pembroke ... to new build that side of the house that fronts the garden with two stately pavilions (towers) at each end, all al Italiano.' The architect was Inigo Jones, who introduced Palladianism to England. The hallmark of the Palladian style was strict adherence to the Greek rules of proportion and symmetry – a kind of classicism par excellence! Jones's **Double-Cube Room** at Wilton is one of the most resplendent rooms in any English house.

Kingston Lacy

Sir John Bankes (1589–1644), a judge and keen supporter of Charles I, bought the estate of Kingston Lacy and the Corfe Castle estate in the 1630s. For six weeks in 1643 his royalist wife, Lady Bankes, famously defended Corfe Castle against 600 Roundheads, but in 1646 Parliamentary gunpowder did lasting damage. The loyalty of the Bankes wasn't forgotten. The son, Sir Ralph Bankes (1631–77) was knighted by Charles II. At Kingston Lacy he built a new house of brick, with Portland stone quoins, a dormered roof and mullioned casement windows. Sir Ralph's house has essentially survived, although a facelift was given in the 1830s by Charles Barry, architect of the New Houses of Parliament.

Levellers and 'True Levellers'

The Levellers were among those for whom puritan rule fell short of the 'Godly' ideal. Their democratic programme, set out in 'The Agreement of the People', incurred the hostility of both Parliament and the army grandees. In May 1649 they revolted.

The Cotswold wool town of **Burford**, whose attractive high street, bordered by stone-built houses, drops sharply downhill, witnessed Cromwell's crushing of the Levellers on the night of 14–15 May. Approaching with his cavalry and dragoons from both ends of the long street, he took the sleeping Levellers by surprise. Only one man was killed on either side, but 340 rebels were taken prisoner. About 500 escaped, but without their horses. The victory was complete. Nothing more was heard of the Leveller programme – Parliament and the army grandees were relieved.

Not, however, for long! The self-styled True Levellers were already digging the soil on **St. George's Hill**, near **Walton-on-Thames** (Surrey). The Diggers (their usual name) believed that everyone had a natural right to use the earth and to enjoy its fruits. They sought a communistic transformation of the 'Godly' commonwealth. 'Work together; eat bread together; declare this all abroad,' the divine voice instructed Gerard Winstanley, the leading Digger. At St. George's Hill, then at **Cobham** (also in Surrey) they challenged the rights of two Lords of the Manor. These and other Digger settlements were eventually dispersed by the forces of the Puritan establishment.

Pendle Hill

In 1652 a young man roughly dressed in leathern breeches, a doublet and a white hat climbed Pendle Hill (Lancs).

'When I was come to the top,' George Fox wrote in his Journal, 'I saw the sea bordering upon Lancashire, and there, on the top, I was moved to sound the day of the Lord, and the Lord let me see in what places He had a great People to be gathered.'

By 1660 this apprentice shoemaker from Fenny Drayton (Leics) had 'gathered a great people', and not only from the north. They included many Levellers, who found in Quakerism a spiritual refuge after their suppression at Burford.

The Sheldonian Oxford

Designed by Sir Christopher Wren, Professor of Astronomy at Oxford, this was the earliest classical building in Oxford. Based on the Theatre of Marcellus in Rome, a structure with three straight sides and the fourth formed in a curve, the huge flat ceiling, suspended from massive beams, is painted with a representation of the sky – which a Roman audience would have seen.

Eyam 1665

The Great Plague of 1665 travelled far and wide. It reached Eyam with a delivery of cloth from the capital. To prevent the spread of the disease, the villagers (about three-quarters of whom died) stayed put. They worshipped at Cucklet Dell, about half a mile from the church.

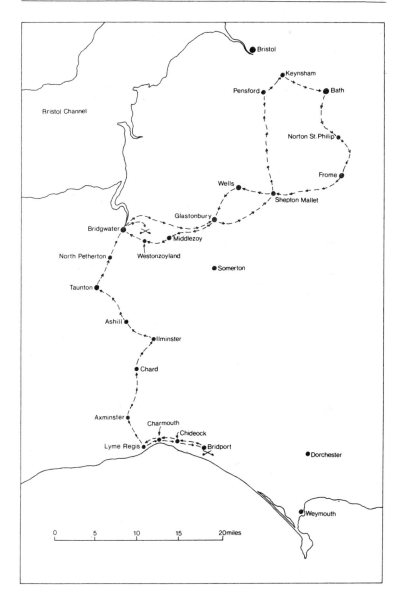

Monmouth's March (David Cheepen)

The Pitchfork Rebellion 1685

Monmouth's Rebellion, which began inauspiciously on 11 June with the landing of three ships near **the Cobb** at **Lyme Regis**, arrived to oust Catholic James II. The Duke's banner declared: 'Fear nothing but God.' The recruits were mainly the yeomen, craftsmen and pitchfork-carrying small farmers of West Dorset and East Devon.

At Bridport the Dorset militia refused to fight the rebels, who returned to Lyme before beginning their long march. At Taunton they crowned the duke king. Amidst the ruins of Glastonbury Abbey they lit their bonfires. On 24 June most of them were climbing the Mendips en route for Bristol, but this great port wasn't attacked, for

Chatsworth House (English Tourist Board)

by now a royal army was in the vicinity. This factor stiffened Bath against surrendering to Monmouth, who moved on to Frome, then west to Wells, where lead from the cathedral roof was converted into bullets. From here he took his men to Bridgewater. In this area farmers called Clubmen were promising support.

On 5 July the Royal army encamped on **Sedgemoor** was taken by surprise when attacked by the rebels. Lord Feversham, the commander, was held up looking for his wig, or so it was said. The young John Churchill took control and Monmouth's host was scattered across the Moor. This was the last battle to be fought on English soil.

The defeated duke rode hard for the Mendips. From here his objective was the Dorset coast, but he got only as far as the Shaftesbury estate. Once arrested, execution awaited him – the fate of anyone who played for the highest stakes and lost.

Many of Monmouth's followers fared as badly. 'Mancatchers' were offered 5s. for every rebel caught. People were scared into confessing in the hope of pardon. On 25th August Lord Chief Justice Jeffrey's Assize opened at Winchester. There ensued a 17th century version of McCarthyism. All 'lying, snivelling Presbyterian Rascals' were connected with 'the late horrid conspiracy,' Jeffreys said. One victim, Dame Alice Lisle, a widow of over 80, accused of harbouring a dissenting minister, was sentenced to be burned. She was later beheaded. Jeffrey's savage court peregrinated through the west country. At Taunton 144 were condemned to hang, and at Wells 99.

Chatsworth House

Frequented by Mary Queen of Scots before her execution at Fotheringhay (Northants) in 1587, the Tudor Chatworth House was begun by Sir William Cavendish, and completed by his widow, the indomitable Bess of Hardwick. In 1686 another William Cavendish, the 4th Earl (later 1st Duke) of Devonshire, and Bess's direct descendant, began to transform the house. The new Chatsworth House was in the Baroque style. Each facade is different – a Baroque feature. The west facade was probably designed by the Duke himself. Spot the sash windows – then an innovative feature.

The History of Myddle

'How comes this happy inclination in the kingdom?
Is it the noise of Camden that has raised men's spirits?'
Edmund Gibson.

A new edition of Camden's survey had just been published when Richard Gough, 'the Sixth Richard of our family', began to write his famous local history (1700). The period saw a small flurry of antiquarian works, possibly inspired by Camden. Gough's debt is barely tangible for, unlike his great predecessor, he recorded the everyday dramas of ordinary folk. From his pages a Salopian soap opera could be constructed!

Myddle lies north of Shrewsbury. Then it was remote, but not cut off. London was about 160 miles away, but Gough records without surprise that his neighbours went there. He himself had visited London in his youth. The landmarks of the village were the church and ruined castle.

Gough drew the seating-plan in the parish church and wrote the family history of each occupant in turn – 'Observations concerning the Seates in Myddle and the familyes to which they belong.' The arrangement formalized the social structure of the parish – the gentry at the front, the yeoman and husbandmen in the middle, and the cottagers at the rear. '...There happened a difference,' Gough recalled, 'beetweene John Downton, of Alderton, and William Formeston, about the right of kneeling in the sixth pew on the south side of the north aisle, and John Downton putt a locke on the pew doore, butt William Formestone, at Marton, who claimed a share in that seate, came on the Lord's day following, and giveing the pew dore a suddaine plucke, broke off the lock.'

The irascible Formeston 'had three sonnes, Thomas, William, and John, and a daughter, named Margarett, who was married to William Challoner of Myddle, cooper. Shee was suspected to bee a light housewife, but never openly defamed; butt shee left three daughters, two of which are as impudent whores as any in this country; one of them has two bastards, and shee being run out of the country they are both maintained by the parish. The other is now (Jan. 20, 1701) great with a bastard, and at Christmas last was sent by order into Wem parish, where her last service and settlement was. She has fathered it on Stephen Formeston, her uncle's son, and hee is fled.'

Life at Myddle could be nasty, brutish and short. James Wycherley was 'endeavouring to come to his mistress, and passing through some out buildings that hee might not bee seene, he gott a fall and broke his thigh and dyed'. Thomas Elks of Knockin murdered a child in a cornfield by putting his head in a pail of water. One girl lived as a servant at Wem, 'att what time a very violent feaver raged there, and comeing home sicke, although shee recovered, yett her father, Rowland Stanway, caught the feaver and dyed, and

Abraham Taylor and his wife comeing often to visit him, gott the feaver and both dyed; and John Taylor, theire son, comeing to see them in theire sicknesse, fell sicke and dyed. These four dyed all in about one month's space....'

In Myddle fortunes were quickly made and lost, as in the case of the owners of Balderton Hall, 'sold five tymes in lytle more than the 100 years last past'. Not even the landscape was unchanging: the park where the castle stood was once wooded, but now – a sign of the times – was being used for pasture.

Castle Howard

Charles Howard, 3rd Earl of Carlisle, who wanted a huge house in the flamboyant Baroque style, offered the architect's job to a young dramatist friend, John Vanbrugh. Vanbrugh enlisted Nicholas Hawksmoor, assistant to Sir Christopher Wren, his task being to add the detail to Vanbrugh's grand design. This is a vast central block, surmounted by a tall dome, between two wings. A great hall, in the shape of a Greek cross, is beneath the dome.

The splendid edifice took from 1700 to 1737 to build. The west wing was built after Vanbrugh's death (in 1726), as were Hawksmoor's **Temple of the Four Winds** and **Mausoleum** for the earl.

Castle Howard (Chris Mountford)

Blenheim Palace

This lavish building was the reward of John Churchill (1st Duke of Marlborough) for defeating the French. Vanbrugh, at the time working on Castle Howard, was appointed architect after meeting Marlborough at the theatre. Queen Anne approved Vanbrugh's designs. Hawksmoor was again involved, and in fact finished the building in the 1720s after Vanbrugh fell out with the irascible duchess, who came to hate him so much that in 1725 she wouldn't allow him into the grounds!

This magnificent building, comparable to the Palace of Versailles, combines baroque and classical features, as does Castle Howard. Arranged around three sides of a huge courtyard, the central block has four turrets and a portico supported by corinthian columns. 'Tis a house, but not a dwelling,' commented Swift, with some justification. Baroque never truly caught on in England, unlike 'homely', yet elegant, classicism.

SOUTH VIEW of BLENHEIM,
The Seat of his Grace the Duke of MARLBOROUGH.

Blenheim Palace (Guildhall Library)

From the 18th Century to the Present

'Indoors and out,' wrote Trevelyan, England in the 18th century 'was a lovely land.' This loveliness was manifested in elegant Georgian architecture, embodying the classical rules of proportion. Reason and decorum were the watchwords of this Age of Elegance. The road of excess, which for Blake led to the Palace of Wisdom, was not generally followed.

Map of England (Generale Kaart von Engeland by J. Ratelband), 1734 (Guildhall Library)

A Georgian Town House (David Cheepen)

Heveningham Hall. Its formal grandeur contrasts with the naturalness of the 'Capability' Brown setting. (David Cheepen)

Bath, where Beau Nash raised decorous living to the level of art, is an enduring reminder of the lifestyle of the favoured, leisured few, for whom taking the medicinal waters was secondary to the playing of a social game governed by rules as fixed as those of Georgian architecture, which at Bath the Royal Crescent famously exemplifies (See p. 175).

The stately home, where privilege could be enjoyed without fear of revolution, or even reproach, mirrored elegance. An example is Heveningham Hall in Suffolk. This Palladian house consists of a central block, with a pedimented wing on either side.

Because elegance and propriety could lead to sterility, there was a reaction against them. The mildly romantic, 'back to nature' longings of the aristocracy explain the phenomenal rise of 'Capability' Brown, who laid out the grounds at Heveningham Hall.

Laurence Brown earned his soubriquet by often remarking, when he viewed the neat and orderly domains of his aristocratic employers, with their manicured yew hedges and walks adorned by statuettes, 'I see great capability of improvement here.' Under Brown's direction, formal gardens were replaced by grass, trees and artificial lakes, the grass and trees going up to the walls of the house.

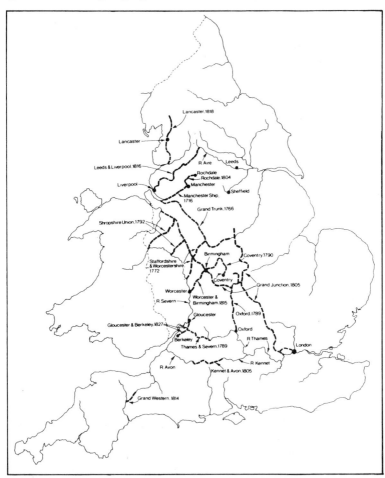

The Canal Age. By enabling goods to be transported cheaply and in bulk, canals served the cause of the Industrial Revolution. However, the slowness of canal transport would be highlighted by the development of railways. (David Cheepen)

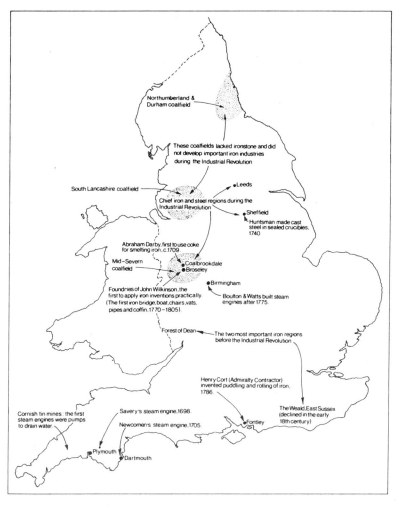

The Industrial Revolution – Iron and Steel (David Cheepen)

At Blenheim, Brown created his largest lake, one befitting Vanbrugh's bridge. In 1776 Boswell communicated his admiration to Dr. Johnson. George III declared that, 'We have nothing equal to this.' The Park was 'one continued galaxy of charming prospects, and agreeably diversified scenes', said a Guide of 1789 – and so it remains.

At Blenheim, the 4th Duke of Marlborough could afford his schemes, but this wasn't always so. In 1754, at Claydon House

159

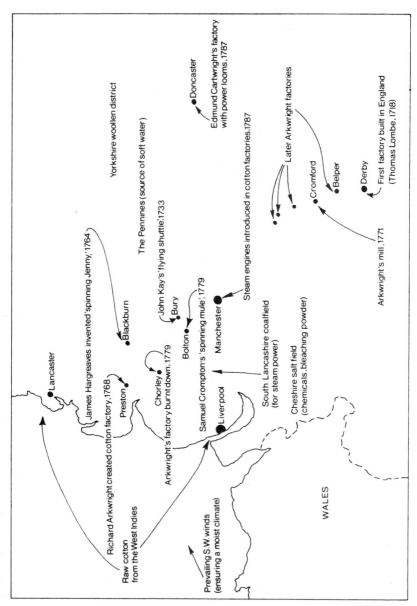

The Industrial Revolution – Textiles (David Cheepen)

(Bucks), Ralph, 2nd Earl Verney started out with a vast fortune. By the time he'd reconstructed and extended his Jacobean manor-house, he was broke, and most of Claydon's contents had to be sold. Verney's legacy includes some of the finest Georgian interiors in England, especially the North Hall, a Palladian double cube, where the pediments of the doorcases are encrusted with Rococo carving.

For men such as Marlborough and Verney, it was axiomatic that their social and political predominance would last for ever. Changes were beginning to take place that would ensure it did not. A New England of textiles, iron, steel and railways was starting to exist alongside the Old England of castles, cathedrals and stately homes. There also took place a transformation of the English countryside, which many of the major landowners helped to bring about.

From the 1750s onwards enclosure proceeded at a startling pace, to produce by c. 1850 a virtually universal chequer-board pattern of much smaller, roughly square fields, hedged by the hawthorn that delights the eye each May. During the same period, over two million acres of common land were enclosed, divided into fields and brought under cultivation. Enclosure was a necessary preliminary to the widespread application of new methods (such as marling of the soil) which promoted the farming efficiency that enabled the demands of the rapidly expanding cities to be met. The agrarian revolution was therefore vital for the emergence of industrial England.

About a hundred years ago, Arnold Toynbee coined the term 'Industrial Revolution' to describe the switch, starting c. 1760, from the small-scale industry of the so-called pre-industrial economy, which ran on a domestic system (producers working in their homes) to one chiefly characterised by large-scale factory production. It would be incorrect to imagine a virtual absence of industry in England prior to c.1760. The Weald of Kent was the centre of a flourishing iron industry long before a dynasty of Quaker ironmasters made Shropshire 'the cradle of the Industrial Revolution'. For this reason some historians have stressed continuity, preferring 'evolution' to 'revolution'. In the 1720s Daniel Defoe toured through England and witnessed economic change: 'New discoveries in metals, mines, minerals; new undertakings in trade; inventions, engines, manufacture....' Nevertheless, if he had repeated his journey in the middle of the 19th century, he would have been in no doubt that a remarkable transformation had occurred. England's first factory – the shape of things to come – was built at Derby in Defoe's time. This was the silk mill built for John and Thomas Lombe in 1718–22. It was about six storeys high, employed 300 men, and was driven by the waterpower of the River Derwent.

It was at Birmingham and Nottingham in the 1760s that the first factories of the Industrial Revolution were established. Matthew Boulton opened his Soho factory in the countryside outside Birmingham in 1765, and here, in partnership with Watt, he would manufacture steam engines. Richard Arkwright erected his first spinning mill, worked by horses, at Nottingham in 1768.

Arkwright is a key figure, the greatest of the new breed of industrial capitalists – the men who in due course would challenge the aristocracy's monopoly of political power. He started life as a barber, travelling around buying hair for wigs. His peregrinations led him to discover the cotton industry, then, due to James Hargreaves' invention of the spinning jenny (1767), starting to boom. With an eye for the main chance, he hired a skilled mechanic to help him construct an improved machine. The mill at Nottingham was a success, so in 1771 he started another at Cromford (Derbys). This one was driven, like the Lombes' silk mill, by the water power of the fast-flowing Derwent. The application of water power to the manufacture of cotton textiles wrought a revolution. The new machinery could only be accommodated in factories, which now spread like wildfire.

The first generation of mills was naturally sited by fast-flowing water. Many were erected at the top of the valleys on either side of the Pennines. Around them villages grew up. Milford, in the Derwent valley, south of Belper, is an example of a later 18th-century industrial village. Here in 1781 the Strutts set up a cotton mill, which still stands. There are cottages, a chapel and a mansion for themselves. At Belper another of their mills also stands to this day.

Men such as Arkwright and the Strutts piled up huge fortunes. Arkwright died worth half a million, the owner of an estate in Herefordshire. Towards their employees they showed an enlightened paternalism, which the village of Milford, with its cottages and chapel, well illustrates. In this, of course, there was more self-interest than philanthropy – contented, healthy workers were likely to be more effective producers. It also reflected the fact that, in the 1770s and 1780s, land was cheap and building materials were abundant.

The development of steam power was indirectly responsible for a dramatic decline in conditions. The coal steam power required blackened and polluted the environment. Factories were no longer located in sequestered spots, but near coalfields or by the newly constructed canals, which brought the coal. Unfortunately, these flat canal-side sites, on which the streets of factory workers' houses grew up, were only drained with difficulty. The resulting sanitary problems created slums. At Milford the Strutts had built their mansion in the village, close to the workers' cottages. By contrast,

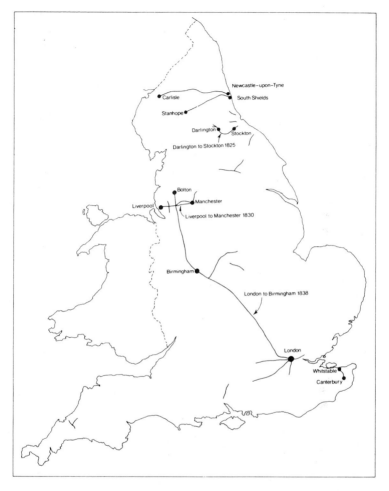

The Railway Revolution – Railway development prior to 1839 (David Cheepen)

the steam age industrialists built theirs far from the begrimed zone of their dark and satanic mills.

Under the impact of industrialisation, small towns, such as Manchester and Birmingham, rapidly expanded. The environmental quality of life declined with equal rapidity. In Liverpool in 1841 expectation of life at birth was 26. This was the stark reality, whether or not (an area of controversy) workers' standard of living rose or fell. In *Hard Times* Dickens describes Coketown as '... a town of

163

machinery and tall chimneys, out of which interminable serpents of smoke trailed themselves for ever and ever, and never got uncoiled'. This portrayal was based upon his observation of Preston, which in 1795 had been 'a handsome, well-built town, with broad regular streets, and many good houses'.*

Celia Fiennes had admired Nottingham for its neatness. She would hardly have recognised it a hundred years on. To the north and south of the city lay over a thousand acres of open fields. The burgesses with co-called Lammas pasture rights – the right to graze cattle or sheep over the open fields after harvesting – refused to allow enclosure, without which not a single house could be built. The self-interest of this 'cowocracy' led to appalling overcrowding within the city's confines. The mushrooming courts and alleys – like the tower blocks of a later age – could accommodate more people in a given space. When enclosure was finally carried through in 1845, it was too late for the immense harm to be reversed.

Hoskins contrasts Nottingham's fortunes with those of Stamford, which Celia Fiennes had also admired. To the north this fair Lincolnshire town was hemmed in by open fields, and to the south by land belonging to the Cecils of Burghley House. In this case it was the Cecils who fulfilled the function of Nottingham's obstructive 'cowocracy'. Apart from preventing building on their own land, they managed to block it on the land they did not own to the north. The fact that slums and overcrowding never materialised was also due to the Cecils, who kept out industry by vetoing the London to York railway line, which instead passed through Peterborough.*

The relationship of the Cecils to Stamford illustrates the political realities of the time. The aristocracy called the tune, and its pre-dominance was reinforced by a corrupt electoral system. At Stamford the Cecils objected to new houses, because these would lessen their political hold. By owning 200 houses, each carrying a vote, they controlled the election of both members. The borough was 'in their pocket'. There were many 'pocket' boroughs. Some were 'rotten' – virtually non-existent. Dunwich, a great port in the Middle Ages, was largely under the sea, but it still returned two M.P.s. So did Old

---

*This description is quoted by Hoskins in his *Making of the English Landscape*.

*The traditional interpretation of this affair has recently been questioned. 'It is no longer clear that the Earl of Exeter actively opposed the building of the line through Stamford, and the reasons for the decision seem to have lain outside of the town, not inside, with Earl Fitzwilliam lobbying Parliament on behalf of Peterborough with great success.' (*The Book of Stamford* Alan Rogers Barracuda Books 1983.) So aristo-cratic influence may still have been decisive in settling the outcome.

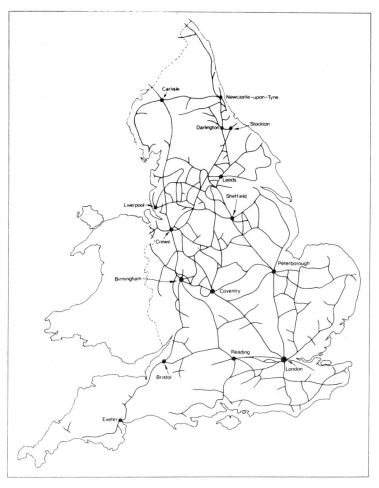

The Railway Mania – the expansion of railways between 1839 and 1852 (David Cheepen)

Sarum, long since superseded by Salisbury's rise. 'Rotten' boroughs were especially amenable to aristocratic control. As a result, many in the Commons were the mouthpieces of the peers who had put them there.

For the vast majority, unrepresented in Parliament, there was no alternative to extra-parliamentary protest, and this could be violent. Luddism, the most famous example, was a direct consequence of the

165

revolution in textiles, which initially took place in spinning. The machine-spun yarn provided plentiful work and high wages for the handloom weavers. This was their Golden Age. When, in the opening years of the 19th century, steam power was applied to weaving, the handloom weavers faced hopeless competition. In desperation they began smashing up the power looms.

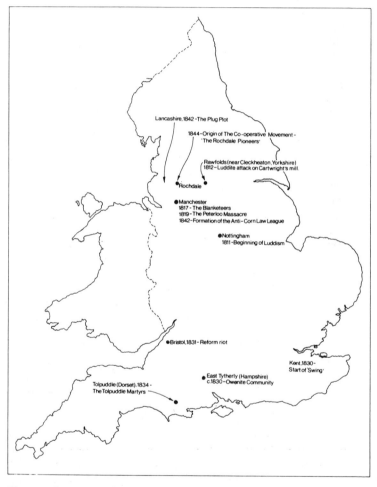

Lancashire, 1842 – The Plug Plot

1844 – Origin of The Co-operative Movement – 'The Rochdale Pioneers'

Rawfolds (near Cleckheaton, Yorkshire) 1812 – Luddite attack on Cartwright's mill.

Rochdale

Manchester
1817 – The Blanketeers
1819 – The Peterloo Massacre
1842 – Formation of the Anti-Corn Law League

Nottingham
1811 – Beginning of Luddism

Bristol, 1831 – Reform riot

Kent, 1830 – Start of 'Swing'

East Tytherly (Hampshire) c. 1830 – Owenite Community

Tolpuddle (Dorset), 1834 – The Tolpuddle Martyrs

Unrest and Protest (c. 1800–c. 1850) (David Cheepen)

'The Reform Bill is a trick – it's nothing but swearing in special constables to keep the aristocrats safe in their monopoly.'

George Eliot 'Felix Holt'

The Great Reform Bill of 1832 swept away the pocket and rotten boroughs. The expanding industrial towns were granted M.P.s for the first time. Middle-class men – the mill-owners, for example – were given the vote. They now ruled the roost with the aristocracy. But ordinary mill workers, and the many like them, were given no stake in the political process. In the 1830s and '40s, they sought a political voice through Chartism, but this mass movement degenerated into sporadic violence. By the end of this period, the masses, unable to improve their position by political means, lived short and unfulfilled lives in grimy, industrial towns, where 'King Cholera' held sway.

At least some people who had power were starting to notice the plight of the powerless. The 'Hungry 40s' as they are called, concentrated able minds. 'The dissolution of mankind into Monads,' wrote Frederick Engels, Manchester mill owner and co-author of *The Communist Manifesto*, 'of which each one has a separate principle, the world of atoms, is here (in the great city) carried out to its utmost extreme....What is true of London is true of Manchester, Birmingham, Leeds....Everywhere barbarous indifference, hard egotism on one hand, and nameless misery on the other....' (*The Condition of the Working Class in England in 1844*.) About the same time, Benjamin Disraeli, a Tory, wrote in *Sybil* of the Two Nations of Rich and Poor. His view of the great cities was similar. Here 'men are brought together by the desire of gain. They are not in a state of co-operation, but of isolation, as to the making of fortunes; and for all the rest they are careless of neighbours. Christianity teaches us to love our neighbour as oneself; modern society acknowledges no neighbour.'

Mid-19th-century England, with its disease-ridden urban chaos, was the product of a movement which had started over a hundred years before in Shropshire and Pennine valleys. Though perhaps less appealing, the mills, canals and railway lines it has left behind are as significant a part of our heritage as the castles, cathedrals and stately homes bequeathed by earlier ages.

By the Diamond Jubilee (1897), 'Two Nations' defined themselves less starkly than in the 1840s. 'King Cholera' had been dethroned, and city streets were gaslit. Life at the mill was still hard, but the length of the working day was now subject to effective legal limitation. All workers had the vote and, because of the Secret

Ballot, they could exercise this hard-won right differently from their bosses. The workhouse certainly cast a shadow, but the public house (a Victorian innovation) offered a sociable consolation!

With their predilection for turning-points, historians may well see one in the Diamond Jubilee. The Victorian 'Age of Improvement' was virtually over. For many in Edwardian England, life would grow harder as real wages declined. In 1909 Lloyd George introduced his People's Budget as 'a war budget. It is for raising money to wage implacable warfare against poverty and squalidness.' For the rich 'nation', however, the Great War was the watershed, for it seemed to sweep away the comfortable world of their pre-war experience – the Edwardian world of elaborate picnics (on which the sun invariably shone) and long weekends at large country houses, where new pluto-crats rubbed shoulders with the traditional aristocracy. Waddesdon Manor (Bucks), built for the Rothschilds in the 1880s, in the style of a French château, conveys the opulence of this period. Many a long weekend was spent here by rising politicians and captains of industry. Edward VII himself was a visitor. In the north-east, the Beamish North of England Open Air Museum offers a more representative impression of early 20th-century lives than Waddesdon Manor.

The declaration of war in August 1914 was greeted with wild enthusiasm, 500,000 volunteering within the first month. *The Times* reported that, 'The generous youth of England has rushed to arms, and the effect upon Oxford and Cambridge is strange indeed. At 11 or noon the streets are not now a-flutter with gowns hurrying to lectures; at 1 o'clock the groups in the gateways are scanty or none. The motor-bicycles are at the front, carrying despatches.'*

The realities of this war were brought home much sooner to the soldiers, than to the towns and villages from which they came. The story of Accrington (Lancs), the smallest borough in the country to raise its own battalion, is especially poignant. On 1 July 1916 700 Accrington Pals, from clubs and pubs, mills and mines, went over the top at the Somme. 585 died in the first hour. At first, when the news was suppressed, anxious crowds besieged the Mayor's house. When the casualty lists were published, their worst fears were confirmed. Almost every family in the town lost a friend or relative. 'Idealism', wrote A.J.P. Taylor, 'perished on the Somme' – this was certainly the case at Accrington.

Shocks could be absorbed more readily by larger communities. It might have seemed that life went on as usual, perhaps at a quickened

*Reports from *The Times* are quoted in *Human Documents of The Lloyd George Era* E. Royston Pike (George Allen and Unwin)

pace. *The Times* reported that ''Busier than usual' is the character-istic boast of Birmingham.' At Liverpool the lights 'shone out with undiminished brilliance in Lime Street'. At Manchester ''High Change' on Tuesdays and Fridays is the crowded and bustling picture it has always been'. Leeds 'has probably never been so pros-perous'. War stimulated demand. 'There is a good deal of homework in these narrow streets of back-to-back houses, where the family washing is hung across the road....' In Sheffield the workmen 'are earning more money than they have ever earned before. Indeed, the only complaint heard is that the men have too little time in which to spend their earnings'.

The war cost England markets in addition to young lives. When, in the autumn of 1933, J.B. Priestley travelled through England, the northern manufacturing towns were in a parlous state. The Slump, heralded by the Wall Street Crash in 1929, had been like a death blow, and it was these industrial communities which bore the brunt. Priestley, himself a Northerner, was angered by what he witnessed: 'For generations, this blackened North toiled and moiled so that England should be rich and the City of London be a great power in the world. But now this North is half derelict, and its people, living on in the queer ugly places, are shabby, bewildered, unhappy....'

Priestley, took an hour's walk in Stockton, where decline was readily apparent. Grass was growing in the shipyards. The big marine engineering shops were empty shells of brick. Many, unemployed for seven and eight years, 'might as well be crossbow-men or armourers, it seems, for all the demand there is for their services. The real town is finished. It is like a theatre that is kept open merely for the sale of drinks in the bars and chocolates in the corridors'.

Hitler had already come to power when Priestley went on his journey. Places like Stockton had him – indirectly – to thank for the economic recovery stimulated by rearmament.

When war broke out with Germany on 3 September 1939, gasmasks were carried, buildings sandbagged, and mothers and children evacuated from towns. When nothing happened, many of them returned before Christmas. This was the period of the Phoney War, which ended in July 1940. The Battle of Britain, fought between July and September, was followed by the winter blitz of 1940–41.

In 1933 Priestley had visited Coventry, where the old and pictur-esque – 'half-timbered and gabled houses that would do for the second act of the *Meistersinger* are besieged by an army of nuts, bolts, hammers, spanners, gauges, drills, and machine lathes, for in a thick ring round this ancient centre are the motor-car and cycle

169

Coventry Cathedral (David Cheepen)

factories, the machine tool makers, the magneto manufacturers, and the electrical companies. Beyond them again are whole new quarters, where the mechanics and fitters and turners and furnace men live in neat brick rows, and drink their beer in gigantic new public houses and take their wives to gigantic new picture theatres.'

Coventry had emerged quickly from the depression. Coal miners, shipbuilders and textile workers from the old industrial areas in the north came in droves to the midlands, where jobs in light industry were available.

On 14 November 1940 this prospering town suffered the first systematic raid of the winter blitz. For ten hours the Luftwaffe rained down their bombs, destroying the historic city centre with its Gothic cathedral. The attack added a new word to the vocabulary of war – 'Coventration', meaning the targeted saturation bombing of a city.

'On every side is a spirit of high adventure, of gay determination, a readiness of experiment, to take reasonable risks, to stake high in this venture of rebuilding our civilisation.' (John Freeman 1945).

The rebuilt Coventry Cathedral, which rose Phoenix-like from the rubble, symbolises the spirit of the immediate postwar years.

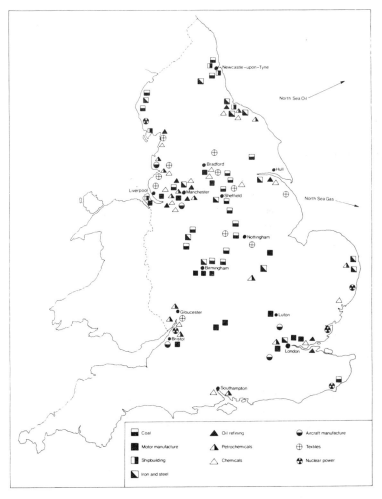

20th-century Industry. The principal centres of traditional, heavy industry are in decline. The burden of this is mainly borne by northern communities. (David Cheepen)

Designed by Sir Basil Spence, and built between 1956 and 62, it stands on the north side of the old cathedral's shell, a porch linking old and new. Graham Sutherland's tapestry, the world's largest, takes the place of an east window. Through the great west screen of clear glass the old cathedral may be seen from inside the new.

171

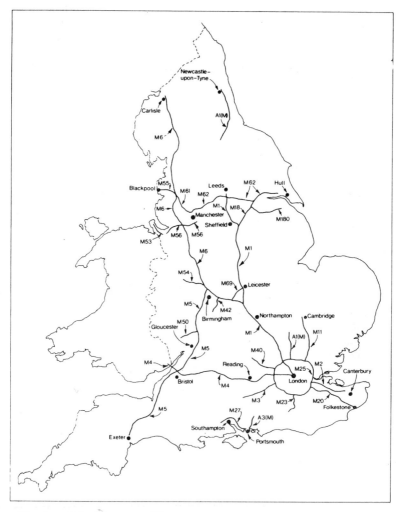

The Age of the Motorway. The M1, England's first motorway, was opened in 1951. The M25, the latest, was finally opened in 1986. (David Cheepen)

Fifty years on, Beryl Bainbridge retraced Priestley's journey through an England once more in the grip of a recession. Priestley had described Stockton as 'finished'. To many this may have seemed the case in July 1983, when unemployment for Stockton and area stood at 16.7% (13,645). Bainbridge wrote that she had never seen

172

'such a godforsaken place in my life. It beggars description, from the mean little park with its scrubby little trees opposite the hotel, to the grim stacks and chimneys and power domes of the ICI chemical works on the horizon. In between, a mess of concrete flats and dingy housing, vulgar precincts and civic centres...'

Further Reading

English Landed Society in the 18th Century G.E. Mingay (Routledge, 1963)

Rural Rides William Cobbett (Penguin, 1967)

The World we have Lost Peter Laslett (University Paperbacks, 1965)

The Industrial Revolution, 1760–1830 T.S. Ashton. (Oxford. New edn pb 1969)

The Making of the English Working Class E.P. Thompson (Penguin, 1963)

Captain Swing E.J. Hobsbawn and G. Rudé (Lawrence and Wishart, 1969)

Victorian England G.M. Young (Oxford, 2nd edn 1960)

Chartist Studies ed. Asa Briggs (Macmillan, 1963)

Victorian Cities Asa Briggs (Penguin, 1968)

English History, 1914–45 A.J.P. Taylor (Oxford, 1965)

The Road to Wigan Pier George Orwell (Left Book Club/Gollancz, 1937. Penguin, 1970)

British Society since 1945 Arthur Marwick (Penguin, 1987)

12 Historic England (5)

Beau Nash and Bath

Camden had recommended Bath's spring water for its 'great vertue to cure bodies overcome and benummed with corrupt humours'. For long, however, the baths were frequented almost solely by the poor. Queen Anne paid a visit in 1702. Three years later, Beau Nash arrived. Even more than the Queen's visit, this was decisive, for the new Master of Ceremonies, ruling with a rod of iron, transformed Bath from a poor and grubby town into an elegant spa, a haven for polite society. An elaborate ritual was enacted, the conventions fixed by Nash, who presided in the Old Assembly Rooms, situated on the east side of the Abbey (now an open space).

Soon to be dignified by the classical architecture of the Woods, Father and Son, and expanding northwards towards Upper Bath, the city becames a visual embodiment of the Georgian ideals of

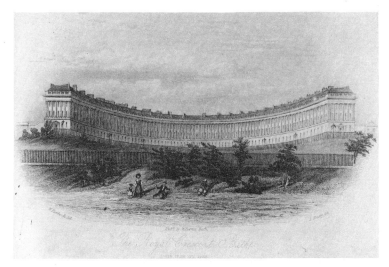

The Royal Crescent, Bath (Guildhall Library)

orderliness and propriety. The masterpiece is the **Royal Crescent** by the younger Wood. His **New Assembly Rooms** were opened in 1771. In the 1790s the **Grand Pump Room** was rebuilt in the classical style.

Beau Nash had died long before this, without seeing the New Assembly Rooms. Though the building went on, nothing was ever quite the same again. Fittingly, a statue of the great M.C. surmounts the clock in the Grand Pump Room.

Mompesson House, Salisbury

Be sure to visit this fine period piece of early 18th-century domestic architecture. It was built by Charles Mompesson, whose initials and coat of arms may be seen on the main facade. Linger in the garden of attractive borders and miniature walks, enclosed on the north side by the old wall of the Cathedral Close.

Ironbridge and the Darbys

Shropshire has been called the cradle of the Industrial Revolution, for it was at Coalbrookdale in the Severn valley that Abraham Darby perfected the smelting of iron with coke. This was in 1709, five

175

The Iron Bridge (English Tourist Board)

years after the Battle of Blenheim – with hindsight, a less momentous event.

The Coalbrookdale ironworks, which would be made by future Darbys into the largest works of any kind in England, produced the first iron wheels, the first iron rails, the first iron boat, the first iron aqueduct, the first iron-framed building and, sited where the small town of Ironbridge would grow up, the world's first iron bridge, built as a showpiece between 1777 and 1781, during the 'reign' of Abraham Darby IV. This dynasty of Quaker ironmasters helped to make England the workshop of the world.

The Ironbridge Gorge Museum, spread over an area of about six square miles, includes:

(1) **The Museum Visitor Centre.**

(2) **Museum of Iron and Old Furnace.**

(3) **Blists Hill Open Air Museum**, a recreation of a Victorian industrial town.

(4) **The Bedlam Furnaces** (constructed 1757).

(5) **The Coalport China Museum** (China was made at the Coalport China Works from the 18th century until 1926).

(6) **The Iron Bridge**.

Cromford (Derbys)*

In this small hamlet Richard Arkwright, wigmaker-turned-industrial capitalist, opened his textile mill, powered by the fast-flowing Derwent. Six storeys high, the mill, though not the water wheel, has survived, as have some of the solid cottages he built for his workers – this was the early, paternalistic phase of the industrial revolution.

Etruria

When Josiah Wedgwood opened his factory at Etruria, near Burslem, the modern pottery industry was born. **Etruria Hall**, which he built to face his new pottery, still stands against a sombre background of colliery tips.

The key to Wedgwood's success was cheap and efficient canal transport, ideal for a fragile commodity. The Grand Trunk Canal, which Wedgwood helped to finance, conveyed Cornish clay, brought by sea to Liverpool or Chester, to the Etruria works, located on its banks. The light finished goods would travel by barge back to Liverpool, or on to Hull.

*See *The Rise and Fall of King Cotton* Anthony Burton (André Deutsch/B.B.C.)

The Royal Pavilion

By the mid-18th century the benefits of sea-bathing were generally recognised. The village of Brighthelmstone began to be transformed into the popular, yet fashionable, resort of Brighton.

The Prince of Wales, the future Prince Regent, paid his first visit in 1783. In July 1786, forced by his debts to close Carlton House, his London residence, he set out again for Brighton, staying for the first time at the house on the Steine, which, on the Prince's orders, would soon be displaced by the Royal Pavilion. Mrs. Fitzherbert, the famous beauty and Roman Catholic, whom he had married secretly in 1785, stayed close by.

For the Prince the architect Henry Holland designed a classical building without flourishes. The central rotunda with wings to north and south forms the nucleus of the Regency extravaganza we see today.

Here, where he would reside every summer and a part of each winter, the dashing Prince would entertain his slightly disreputable friends, such as Beau Brummell. And here, very briefly, he lived with Princess Caroline of Brunswick, whom he married in 1795 in return for the King settling his debts. The cynical arrangement produced a

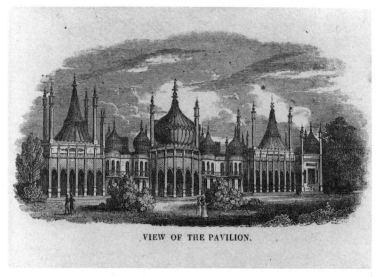

VIEW OF THE PAVILION.

The Royal Pavilion, Brighton (Guildhall Library)

child (Princess Charlotte, born in January 1796) and was then terminated. In 1800 the Prince and Mrs. Fitzherbert, for whom a new house (still standing) was built on the Steine, got back together. It was a mercy for them that the disapproving George III preferred Weymouth!

In 1811, when the King went finally mad, the Prince became Prince Regent. Brighton became the centre of Regency civilisation – almost a second capital.

The Prince Regent appointed John Nash (no relation of Beau) as his Surveyor-General. Under the Prince's direction, Nash designed the splendid oriental exterior with its eye-catching array of pinnacles and minarets.

The oriental spirit had been abroad for some time. At the Royal Pavilion the Chinese style had already entered the interior, notably in the **Chinese Gallery** (1802). When the Prince contemplated the enlargement of the Pavilion, it was (with the idea of complementing these interior schemes) a Chinese exterior he first considered. Then the Prince was converted to the Indian, Islamic form of Orientalism. Nash was the second to come up with an Indian scheme, the first being Humphrey Repton, the landscape gardener.

The Pavilion was near to completion when the Prince Regent at last ascended the throne (1820). The new King went on coming. In June 1830 he died, disliked by almost everybody. Indeed, the Monarchy did well to survive him. The style of the Royal Pavilion would not be imitated in England. Nor, incidentally, would the style of George IV!

Coke of Norfolk and Holkham Hall

William Kent designed Holkham Hall for Thomas Coke (1697–1759). The grandeur of this palladian mission, around which the Park was created, is best appreciated from the south, the direction from which visitors (travelling from London and Newmarket) were intended to approach.

Holkham's famous association is with Thomas William Coke, 'Coke of Norfolk' (1752–1842), a pioneer of the Agrarian Revolution. Inheriting the estates in 1776, his influence spread through the progressive example he gave to his tenants. Coke's practice of 'marling' (digging the underlying marl and spreading it over the sandy topsoil) converted unproductive land into rich prairie – so Arthur Young, that tireless traveller and seasoned observer of new farming techniques, was able in 1804 to write: 'Now the most abundant crops of wheat and barley cover the entire district'. The annual sheep shearings Coke organised at Holkham attracted not only the tenantry, but all those interested in agriculture. The monument, a 120 foot column, the south side of which shows a Holkham sheep shearing, was erected by public subscription in 1845.

Wimpole Hall (Cambs)

The central block, eventually refaced, of Cambridgeshire's finest stately home dates from 1640–70, when Sir Thomas Chicheley, a friend of Wren, built the first house. With later developments, two great architects, Sir James Gibbs and Sir John Soane, were closely associated.

In the early 18th century, Gibbs designed the west wing, chapel and library. The **Chapel** was decorated by Sir James Thornhill, also renowned for his ceilings at Blenheim, Greenwich and St. Paul's. The magnificent **Library** was built to accommodate the collection of Edward Harley, 2nd Earl of Oxford, the owner of Wimpole Hall.

Harley's passion for building outrunning his means, he was forced to sell Wimpole to Philip Yorke, 1st Earl of Hardwicke, the famous Lord Chancellor. The Harleian Collection, which was also sold off, helped to establish the British Museum.

The 1st Earl had the central block refaced by Henry Flitcroft. The 2nd called in the ubiquitous 'Capability' Brown to extend the park to the north. Brown built the Gothic tower – the fashion for 'things medieval' was starting to grow – and made a series of lakes between this and the house. For the 3rd Earl, who succeeded in 1790, Sir John Soane, a personal friend, designed the domed **Yellow Drawing Room**, no less fine than Gibb's Library, and also the **Book Room** and **Bath House**.

Under the direction of the 3rd Earl, as passionate an agrarian improver as Coke of Norfolk, Wimpole became a centre of enlightened agriculture. The farm buildings were also designed by Soane. The **Barn**, the most important of these, now sets out the history of farming on the estate.

Wordsworth and the Lakes

'Fair seed-time had my soul, and I grew up
Foster'd alike by beauty and by fear;
Much favour'd in my birthplace, and no less
In that beloved vale to which, erelong,
I was transplanted'.

From 'The Prelude'

At the end of 1799, the young Wordsworth returned to the scenes of his childhood and early youth. His **birthplace**, now owned by the National Trust, is in the main street of Cockermouth. At Hawkshead, where he attended the **Grammar School**, he lodged at **Ann Tyson's Cottage**. Both school and cottage survive – as does the poet's name carved on a desk!

William and Dorothy made their home close to Grasmere, the roundest of the lakes. The village is about $\frac{1}{4}$ mile north of the lake, west of the Keswick Road, on the east side of which, at Town End, Dove Cottage is situated. Coleridge would think nothing of striding over the Fells to Dove Cottage from Keswick.

By this time the Fells were becoming popular. Previously they had aroused hostility or indifference. In the 1720s Defoe referred to their 'inhospitable terror'. In his journal of 1769 (published in 1775) Thomas Gray dismissed the Cumberland hills as 'of no use or advantage either to man or beast'.

The situation was transformed by the advent of guide books. 'Lakers' came to explore what others described. Though he disliked them, Wordsworth himself wrote a guide book. His *Guide to the Lakes*, which was read more widely than his poems, attracted still more visitors.

Dove Cottage, where Wordsworth wrote the Prelude, wasn't his home for long. In 1808 he moved out with his growing family, and Thomas de Quincey moved in. In search of space, they came first to Allan Bank, north-west of the church, and later to the Parsonage. In 1813 they left Grasmere for roomy **Rydal Mount** (N.T.), overlooking Rydal Water.

Here Wordsworth grew old and crusty. Continuing to dislike visitors, he was appalled by the construction of the Kendal and Windermere Railway. The poor, he wrote, wouldn't benefit 'mentally or morally' from the Lakes. What his opinion would be of the cars and caravans of the 1980s, is not difficult to imagine.

Dove Cottage (English Tourist Board)

William Cobbett's Rural Rides

In the 1820s William Cobbett travelled far and wide, observing a countryside being rapidly transformed by enclosure. Always sympathetic towards the 'small man', he didn't find this development congenial. Though he'd made his name as a Tory critic of Tom Paine, long before the 1820s he had come to despise the entire political and social system, which he called 'The Thing'. Its opportunities for profiteering and corruption allowed parasites to prosper while the producers, often landless, due to enclosure, struggled to survive. Cobbett denounced the present while yearning for a partly imaginary past of contented, self-sufficient peasants cultivating their strips in the open fields.

Rural Rides is both the record of journeys and a polemic against 'The Thing' in all its manifestations. On 11 September 1826 Cobbett was travelling through Wiltshire, en route for Malmesbury, where the abbey ruins would evoke the memory of St. Aldhelm.

'Here are some of the very finest pastures in all England, and some of the finest dairies of cows, from 40 to 60 in a dairy, grazing in them ... and there were formerly two churches here, where there is now only one, and five, six or ten times as many people. I saw in one single farmyard here more food than enough for four times the inhabitants of the parish ... but, while the poor creatures that raise the wheat and the barley and cheese and the mutton and the beef are living upon potatoes, an accursed Canal comes kindly through the parish to convey away the wheat and all the good food to the tax-eaters and their attendants in the WEN!'

The Tolpuddle Martyrs

'I am not sentencing you for any crime you have committed, or that it could be proved that you were about to commit, but as an example to the working classes of this country!

Judge John Williams, Dorchester Assizes, 19 March 1834.

'The sentence as regards these poor deluded men seems to us too severe, but it may be useful if it spreads alarm....'

The Times

'I believe that nothing will ever be done to relieve the distress of the working classes, unless they take it into their own hands. With these views I left England, and with these views I am returned.'

George Loveless

When six Dorsetshire labourers (including Loveless) formed a local branch of an agricultural union, affiliated to Robert Owen's G.N.C.T.U. (Grand National Consolidated Trade Union), they were arrested, taken to Dorchester (a distance of seven miles), and there, on a charge of illegal oath-taking, put on trial.

The Prosecution based its case on an act of 1797, when the country was at war with France, and potential mutineers sometimes bound themselves by secret oaths. Judge Williams ruled that its provisions could apply to farm workers in peacetime. Unwisely, the labourers had adopted an initiation procedure involving blindfolding and the picture of a skeleton on the wall, and this played into the prosecution's hands.

The real issue, as the Judge himself states, was not the imagined infringement of an existing law. He had witnessed the French Revolution at first hand. Only four years before, in the so-called Swing Movement, mobs in the southern and eastern counties had been smashing threshing machines. He was taking no chances with these six. Behind him the guiding hand of Lord Melbourne, the Prime Minister, may be discerned. A harsh sentence was imposed of seven years transportation.

One labourer, named James Hammett, allowed himself to be mistaken for his brother, John, whose wife was expecting a baby. He too was transported.

A Government pardon came when the Martyrs had served just a fraction of their sentence. All of them returned to England, but only Hammett stayed here. He died in 1891 in the workhouse at Dorchester, and lies buried in the churchyard at Tolpuddle.

A Brunel Trail

Fearful of revolution, Wellington opposed the advent of railways because they would 'encourage the lower classes to move about'. The Iron Duke was thankfully ignored. From 1830, which saw the opening of George Stephenson's Manchester and Liverpool line, the Railway Revolution gathered steam.

Canals had kept close to the waterways. The railways penetrated parts of the country they could not reach. The process came to a head in the speculative bonanza of the Railway Mania. By 1852 (the year of Wellington's death) almost all the main lines of the modern network had been laid. Towns such as Crewe had sprung up, whose sole *raison d'être* was the railways.

The navvies ('inland navigators'), who toiled, and often died, to

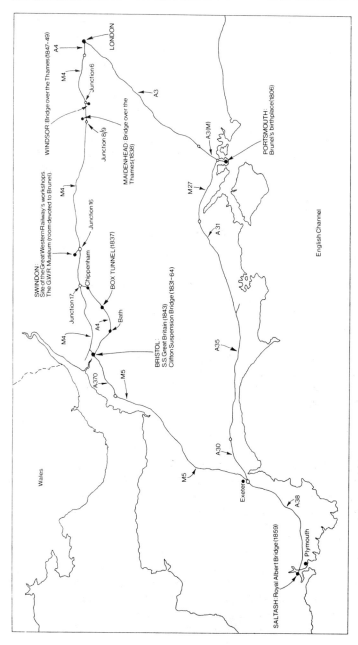

A Brunel Trail (David Cheepen)

enable the lower classes to move about, were the heroes of the Railway Age, while Brunel was the colossus bestriding it.

Born to an engineering father, Sir Marc (the first to tunnel under the Thames), the talent of Isambard Kingdom developed early. When, at the age of 27, he was appointed engineer to the projected Great Western Railway, he was famous locally for designing the **Clifton Suspension Bridge**. With scant regard for tradition, he adopted a broad gauge of 7′ 0¼″, though everywhere else it was 4′ 8½″. With a name like his, he could get away with such iconoclasm.

The Broad Gauge has not survived, but much else of Brunel's has. He designed the **Box Tunnel**, between Chippenham and Bath, as a special memorial to himself. On 9 April, his birthday, the sun shines through the tunnel from end to end.

Seebohm Rowntree's York

Rowntree, a Quaker manufacturer, was one of the first to record poverty scientifically. In 1899 he discovered that about 30% of the citizens of York, a more prosperous town than many, were living in poverty. By his definition, families were poor 'whose total earnings are insufficient to obtain the minimum necessaries for the maintenance of merely physical efficiency'. He concluded: 'The wages paid for unskilled labour in York are insufficient to provide food, clothing and shelter adequate to maintain a family of moderate size in a state of bare physical efficiency.'

When Rowntree repeated his survey in 1936, he found that the grinding poverty of low-paid wage-earners had gone, but, due to un-employment, poverty was still for many a basic fact of life.

Rowntree's last survey (1951) showed that the percentage in poverty had dramatically declined. He deduced that the problem of poverty had been largely solved. ('Most of our people,' said Harold Macmillan in 1957, 'have never had it so good.')

Hardy's Wessex

Thomas Hardy's idyllic **birthplace** at **Higher Bockhampton** was built by his grandfather on the edge of heathland. In a room upstairs, he did much of his early writing, including *Far from the Madding Crowd* (1874). A bestseller, serialised in the prestigious *Cornhill Magazine*, it made possible the move to **Max Gate**, a mile from Dorchester, a mansion which Hardy (an architect by training)

Hardy's Birthplace (English Tourist Board)

himself designed. He wrote *The Mayor of Casterbridge* while supervising the building.

Here, in circumstances removed from the rustic simplicities he depicted, Hardy would live till his death in 1928 – over forty years after the publication of his last novel *Jude the Obscure.*

Corresponding in area – or so Hardy believed – to Alfred's Kingdom, the Wessex of his novels and poems combines fact and fiction – a detailed correlation with the actual map is not therefore possible.

The broad brush strokes are clear – Higher and Lower Bockhampton are combined with the parish of Stinsford to make Mellstock, the nucleus of Hardy's Wessex.

187

> *'William Dewy, Tranter Reuben, Farmer Ledlow late at plough,*
> *Robert's Kin, and John's, and Ned's,*
> *And the Squire, and Lady Susan, lie in Mellstock*
>   *churchyard now!'*

In the churchyard at Stinsford, Hardy's heart was buried.

Dorchester becomes *Casterbridge*. Lulworth Cove is thinly disguised as *Lulstead Cove*, where in *Far From The Madding Crowd*, Troy is carried out to sea. *Egdon Heath* is a composite of several tracts of heathland, including the (now conifer clad) heath around Higher Bockhampton. Oxford, on the periphery of Wessex, is dignified as *Christminster*, where Jude laboured in proximity to the forever inaccessible groves of academe.

Jarrow 1987. The bleak landscape might be almost anywhere. The shipyard cranes of this historic – and symbolic – town dominate the background. Events here led to the Jarrow March. At that time Jarrow's infantile mortality was 112 per thousand births, about twice the national rate. This is also the town of Bede. Remains of his monastery's cloister may still be seen. Parts of his monastic church survive as the chancel of the parish church. Today Jarrow shares with other towns the demoralising effects of recession. (Chris Mountford)

Jarrow

The town where, in the time of Bede, 'the river ran, a clear stream, through a green valley' now 'looked as if it had entered a perpetual penniless bleak Sabbath'. This was Priestley's view of Jarrow in the wake of the slump, when the closure of Palmer's shipyard had thrown thousands on the dole. 69% of 'Red Ellen' Wilkinson's constituents were unemployed. 'The men,' wrote Priestley, 'wore the drawn masks of prisoners of war.'

Three years on, many were marching to London. 'I have suffered hardships for many years...,' said one, aged 60. 'Nothing that can happen on the road between here and London can be worse.'* This marcher was dead within a month.

Following Priestley's route, Beryl Bainbridge visited Jarrow in 1983. 'Who,' she asked, 'could have foreseen that the slow process of change would accelerate to an extent not experienced since the Industrial Revolution, wiping away buildings and traditions and values in the twinkling of an eye, and that the sum total of such momentous changes would amount in the end to no more than a modern version of that earlier, bleak Sabbath of a hole, with a shopping precinct and a dole-office called by another name...?'

Churchill and Chartwell

Winston Churchill acquired Chartwell in 1923. The house commands a fine prospect over the Weald of Kent. 'I bought Chartwell for that view,' he said in later years.

At his Kentish retreat, Churchill found an outlet – one especially useful in the Wilderness Years of 1929–39 – for his phenomenal energy. 'I built with my own hands a large part of the cottages and extensive kitchen-garden walls, and made all kinds of rockeries and waterworks and a large swimming pool.... Thus I never had a dull or idle moment from morning to midnight, and with my happy family around me dwelt at peace within my habitation.'

When Chancellor of The Exchequer (1925–29), Churchill was already busy with his bricklaying. 'The greater part of this wall,' declares a tablet in the east wall, 'was built between the years 1925 and 1932 by Winston with his own hands.' (The kitchen-garden beyond was grassed over in 1966.)

In the 30s Churchill did far more at Chartwell than lay bricks.

*Quoted in *The Long March of Everyman 1750–1960*. Edited by Theo Barker (Penguin)

Chartwell (English Tourist Board)

Here he wrote the great biography of Marlborough, his ancestor, for whom he felt an affinity. He had been born at Blenheim Palace, and in the churchyard at nearby Bladon, he would be buried.

Churchill's political involvement didn't cease at this time. At Chartwell his 'little Foreign Office', reporting back on developments in Germany, furnished ammunition for speeches in the House.

In the War years, the Premier would sometimes sneak down to Kent. On these occasions, the house being closed, he would stay in one of the cottages he himself had built. Alone here, in 1941, he received news of Wavell's abortive attack on Rommel in the Western Desert.

Defeated in the 1945 election, Churchill settled down at Chartwell to write a 12 volume history of the War. In 1951, now in his late 70s, he was returned to No. 10. Not till 1954, following retirement at eighty, would he have time to enjoy to the full the view over the Weald of Kent.

Milton Keynes

'There was, first, Old England, the country of the cathedrals and minsters. . . . Then, I decided, there is the nineteenth-century England, the industrial England . . . . The third England, I concluded, was the new post-war England, belonging far more to the age itself than to this particular island. America, I supposed, was its real birthplace. . .'

J.B. Priestley 'English Journey' 1933.

'A series of motorways circled by endless roundabouts, with the houses hidden behind clumps of earth', was how Beryl Bainbridge described England's largest planned urban development, inaugurated in 1967 to accommodate London's population overspill.

The grand design, like much else in 20th-century England, was derived from an American model. Its assumption was that everybody would be employed, prosperous and able to drive to work. The grid road system links scattered new estates with (three) absorbed towns, and (thirteen) villages. East-west roads (H1 to H10) are called 'Ways'. Those running north-south are called 'streets', and are coded VI–VII. Like the new estates, employment areas are dotted around the city, partly to avoid traffic jams.

In Central Milton Keynes, the bright and airy shopping precinct is landscaped with trees and shrubs. There's even a fountain. Bainbridge was told to think of 'this glittering hall of glass as a church, a cathedral dedicated to the worship of the credit card'. Disliking Milton Keynes, she thought that – had it existed in 1933 – Priestley would have made a detour round it. He did have a romantic distaste for the 'Third England', which Milton Keynes represents, though it was 'a cleaner, tidier, healthier, saner world than that of 19th-century industrialism'.

Straight roads, consumerism and the famous – or infamous – **concrete cows** are not the whole story, for Old England co-exists with the New. Monks Way leads to the remains of **Bradwell Abbey**, which include a 14th century **Chapel** (open for visitors on the last Sundays of June, July and August).

The past is more than just tolerated – it is consciously blended with the present. For example, at **Stony Stratford**, one of the incorporated towns, where in 1483 Duke Richard waylaid Edward V and the Woodvilles, a modern shopping and office centre has been styled in the town's traditional manner.

13 Population

P opulation levels prior to 1801, the year of the first census, are arrived at by informed guesses. Where information is scarce, estimates vary most widely. It is lacking for pre-Roman England, which, given recent questioning of the picture of lowland areas covered by forest, with settlement restricted to the uplands, was possibly less sparsely populated than has been imagined.

An estimated figure for the period of Roman occupation is c.3 or 4 million, higher than at the time of Domesday.

The Domesday Survey – the nearest thing to a census before 1801 – covers the population spectrum from the lord in his manor to the slave on the demesne. The recorded population (c.275,000) refers only to the heads of households. A multiplier of five, corresponding to the likely average size for a medieval family, brings the total to c.1½ million.

The population of England more than doubled between 1086 and the start of the 14th century, when it probably reached c.4 million. The turning point was not, as it is often assumed, the Black Death, but the less recalled famines of 1315–17 and 1321. These were the result of population growth outstripping the means of subsistence. Famine left the poor vulnerable to countless 'pestilences'.

When the Black Death arrived in 1348, it struck an already weakened and declining population, now reduced by at least a third. The towns, ports especially, were worst affected. At Bristol mortality was between 35% and 40%. At York, a busy port at this time, it was 32%.

Demographic recovery was under way in the 15th century, and was progressing fast, though not in every area, by the start of the 16th. An example of a growth region, partly due to the new iron industry, was the Weald of Kent. This had been sparsely populated in the 14th century.

Towns spilled out beyond their walls. By 1600 linear surburbs extended from York (pop. c.12,000) on all sides. Though the north's foremost city, its days as a great port (with Hull, closer to the sea, on

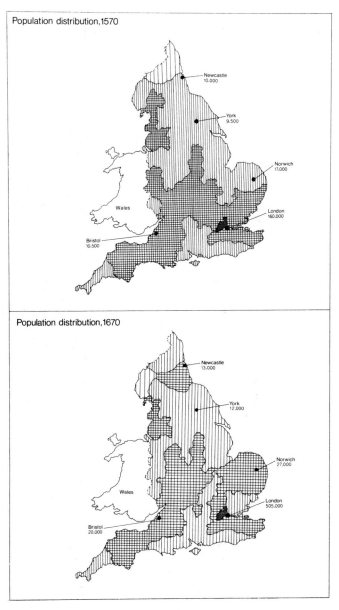

Population distribution, 1570

Newcastle
10.000

York
9.500

Norwich
17.000

Wales

London
160.000

Bristol
10.500

Population distribution, 1670

Newcastle
13.000

York
12.000

Norwich
27.000

Wales

London
505.000

Bristol
20.000

Population distribution, 1570 and 1670 (David Cheepen)

193

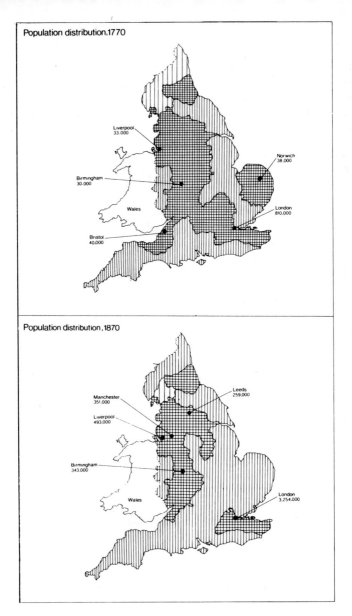

Population distribution, 1770 and 1870. Dark squares indicate a greater density of population. Each map also shows the five largest cities. It may be seen that the most dramatic changes occur within the period 1770 and 1870, by which time Manchester and Leeds have taken the places of Norwich and Bristol, and our modern spread has been reached. (David Cheepen)

the ascendant) were numbered. Bristol (pop. c.12,000) had long since burst the bounds of its medieval walls. 'For trade of merchandize,' it was 'a second London, and for beauty and account next unto York,' wrote Speed, the celebrated mapmaker, about this time. Norwich (pop. c.15,000) housed more than either of these, and, unlike them, was still virtually contained within its medieval walls. Industrial centres such as the clothing towns of Halifax, Leeds and Wakefield, and Sheffield (pop. c.2,200) were emerging. Down south, as many houses in Colchester, a cloth town (pop. c.5,000), were standing 'without the walls' as within, and this was typical of many smaller, prospering provincial towns.

Estimates of England's population in 1600 vary from 3.6 to 5 million. By now the rate of growth was decreasing in most areas.

In 1695 Gregory King calculated that the level had risen to 5.5 million. John Rickman, who supervised the 1801 census, arguing backwards from the parish registers, concluded that there was another million by 1750.

Then the rate of population growth began to rise, accelerating sharply after 1780. A falling death rate and a rising birth rate have both been advanced as explanations of this population explosion, which has been seen as both a cause and an effect of the Industrial Revolution.

The 1801 Census recorded a population in England of 8,331, 434. Though the Industrial Revolution was in full swing, only 19% of the people lived in towns of more than 20,000 inhabitants. Population would continue to increase, as would the process of urbanisation. (The Census of 1851 recorded that England was inhabited by 16.9 million people. This figure had doubled by 1911, and tripled by 1981.)

Further Reading

A New Historical Geography of England Edited by H. C. Darby (C.U.P. 1973)

Village and Farmstead: a History of Rural Settlement in England C. Taylor (George Philip, 1983)

Interpreting the Landscape (especially chapter 12) M. Aston (Batsford, 1985).

14 Famous Addresses

CHARLES DARWIN	Down House (Kent) nr. Sevenoaks. Open daily, except Mon. and Fri.
GENERAL WOLFE	Quebec House (Westerham, Kent) (N.T.) Open daily, except Thurs. and Sat. March to Oct: 2–5 or 6.
THE YOUNGER PITT	Pitt's Cottage (Westerham, Kent). Restaurant.
VICTORIA SACKVILLE-WEST and HAROLD NICOLSON	Sissinghurst Castle (Kent) nr. Ashford (N.T.) Open daily.
RUDYARD KIPLING	Batemans (Sussex) nr. Heathfield (N.T.) Mon. to Thurs. 2–6. Also (June to Sept.) 11–12.30.
LEONARD AND VIRGINIA WOOLF	Monk's House (Rodmell, Sussex). Open daily.
BERNARD SHAW	Shaw's Corner (Ayot St. Lawrence, Herts) nr. Hitchin (N.T.) Open daily, except Tues. (closed Dec. and Jan.)
JOHN MILTON	Milton's Cottage (Chalfont St. Giles, Bucks). Open daily except Tues. (Nov. to Jan. only at weekends).
BENJAMIN DISRAELI	Hughenden Manor (Bucks) nr. High Wycombe (N.T.) Open Wed. to Sat 2–6, Sun. 12–6. Closed Nov. to March.
THE ASTORS	Cliveden (Bucks) nr. Marlow (N.T.) House: Apr. to Oct. Thurs. and Sun. 3–6. Grounds: Mar. to end Dec: daily 11–6.
JANE AUSTEN	Chawton (Hants) nr. New Alresford. Open daily.
EARL MOUNTBATTEN OF BURMA	Broadlands (Romsey, Hants).
T.E. LAWRENCE	Clouds Hill (Dorset) nr. Wimborne (N.T.) Apr. to Sept: Wed. to Fri and Sun. 2–5. Oct. to Mar: Sun. only 1–4.

SIR EDWARD ELGAR	Upper Broadheath (Worcs) nr. Worcester. Birthplace. Cottage open daily.
TOM PAINE	Thetford (Norfolk). Birthplace. Cottage (tablet) behind White Hart St.
SIR ROBERT WALPOLE	Houghton Hall (Norfolk) nr. King's Lynn. Mid Apr. to late Sept: Thurs. and Sun. 2–5.
THE BRONTES	The Parsonage (Haworth, Yorks) nr. Keighley. Open daily. Sun. from 2.
JOHN RUSKIN	Brantwood (Coniston, Lancs). Mon. to Fri. 10–4.30. Sat from 2.30.
BEATRIX POTTER	Hill Top (nr. Sawrey, Cumbria) nr. Hawkeshead. (N.T.) Easter to Oct: weekdays 11–5.30. Sun. from 2.
GEORGE STEPHENSON	Wylam-on-Tyne (Northd) (N.T.) Birthplace. 1 room only open Wed. Thurs. Sat. and Sun. 2–5.

15 Fifteen Tours of Historic England

England's supply of castles and cathedrals, historic towns and stately homes could have kept my toiling mapmaker from his painting for many years. The relatively small sample in my proposed tours are featured in the Historic England section (1–5). The bracketed numbers refer to these. Use the index on p. 239 to find information quickly.

Don't neglect the minor roads. Good travelling!

N.B. The maps only cover essentials. I suggest they are supplemented by a Great Britain Road Atlas.

I strongly recommend membership of both the National Trust (36 Queen Anne's Gate, London SW1H 9AS) and of English Heritage (Fortress House, Savile Row, London W1X ZHE). In this way you both support good causes and, since membership provides free entry to their properties, save money.

N.B. (i) Properties are generally open on the Spring and Summer Bank Holidays.
 (ii) Where no opening times for sites are stated, access at any reasonable time may be assumed.

TOUR 1

London – Windsor – Eton

Windsor Castle (3) Lower Ward open daily 10–4. Round Tower open Apr. to Sept. 10–1, 2–3.45. St. George's Chapel open (except Jan.) 11–3 or 4 (Fri. from 1, Sun. from 2 or 2.15).

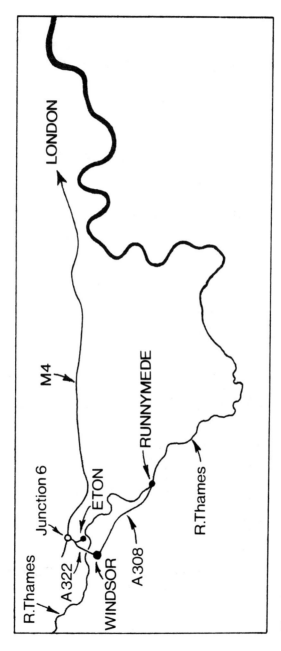

Tour 1 – Route (David Cheepen)

Eton College (3)   School Yard and Cloisters may be visited from 12 (from 2 in summer), from 10 in holidays. Guided tours (charge) of Chapel, Upper School and Lower School available 11.30 (10.30 in holidays) – 12.30 and 2.30–5, or 2–6. College closed Sun.

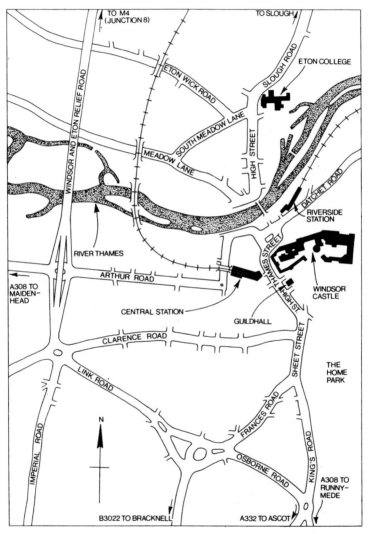

Windsor and Eton – Sketch Map (David Cheepen)

TOUR 2

London – Brighton – Alfriston – Bodiam Castle

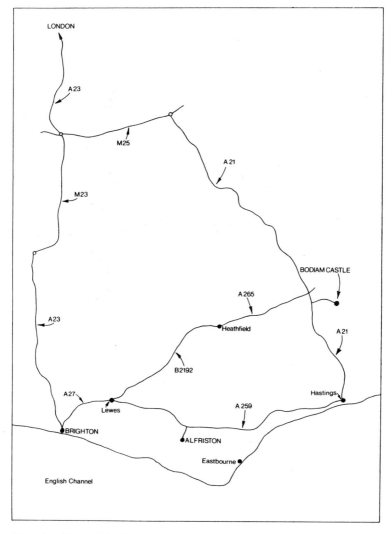

(Tour 2 – Route) (David Cheepen)

The Royal Pavilion Open daily. Charge
(5)

The Clergy House, Open daily Apr. to Oct. Charge
Alfriston (3) N.T.

Bodiam Castle (3) Open daily. Weekends only Oct. to March. Charge
N.T.

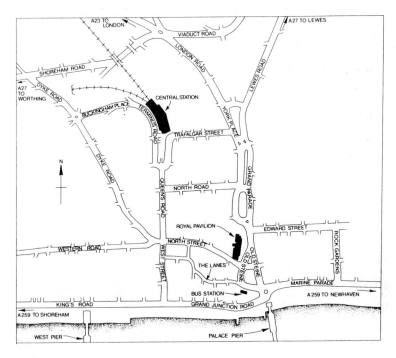

Brighton – Sketch Map (David Cheepen)

TOUR 3

London – Oxford – Blenheim Palace – Burford – Chedworth – Cirencester –
Avebury

Merton College Oxford (3)   Library open 2–4 or 5

Christ Church (4)

The Bodleian (4)   Open daily (except Sun.) Sat. 9.30–12.30

The Sheldonian (4)   Open daily

Blenheim Palace (4)   Open daily mid-March to Oct. Charge

Burford (4)

Chedworth (Roman villa) (2) N.T.   Open daily (except Mon.) Closed Jan. and 1st half Oct. Charge

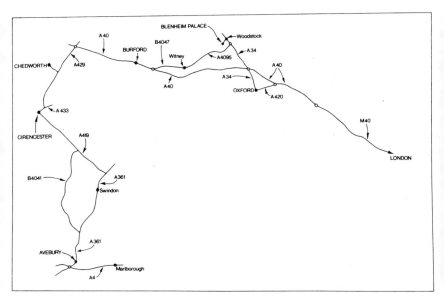

Tour 3 – Route (David Cheepen)

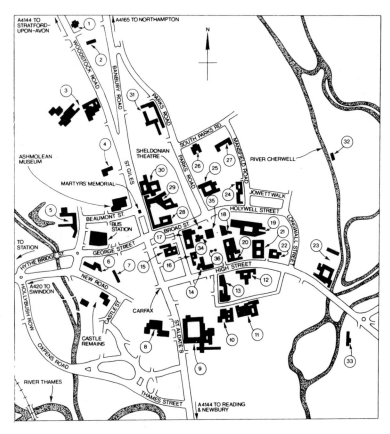

Oxford – Sketch Map (David Cheepen)

1. St. Anthony's College
2. St. Anne's College
3. Somerville College
4. Regent's Park College
5. Worcester College
6. Nuffield College
7. St. Peter's College
8. Pembroke College
9. Christ Church College
10. Corpus Christi College
11. Merton College
12. University College

13. Oriel College
14. Brasenose College
15. Jesus College
16. Lincoln College
17. Exeter College
18. Hertford College
19. New College
20. All Souls's College
21. Queens' College
22. St. Edmund Hall
23. Magdalen College
24. Manchester College

25. Wadham College
26. Rhodes House
27. Mansfield College
28. Balliol College
29. Trinity College
30. St. John's College
31. Keble College
32. St. Catherine's College
33. St. Hilda's College
34. Divinity School
35. Bodleian Library
36. Radcliffe Camera

**Corinium Museum
(Cirencester) (2)**   Open daily (except Mon. in Winter) Sun. from 2

**Amphitheatre (2)
(English Heritage)**

**Avebury (1)
(Eng. Heritage)**   Museum open daily

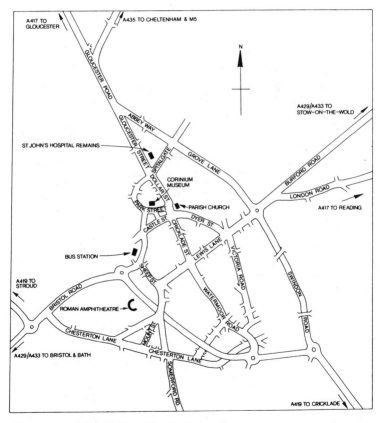

Cirencester – Sketch Map (David Cheepen)

TOUR 4

London – Knole – Ightam Mote – Chartwell – Hever Castle – Penhurst Place – Leeds Castle.

Knole (4) (N.T.) Open Wed. to Sat. Sun. 2–5. Closed Dec. to Feb. Charge

Ightam Mote (3) Open daily (except Tues. and Sat.) Apr. to Oct. Charge

(N.T.)

Chartwell (5) (N.T.) House open Sat., Sun and Wed. (March and Nov.), Tues., Wed., Thurs., Sat., Sun. (Apr. to Oct). Garden and Studio: Apr. to Oct. (same times) Charge

Hever Castle (4) Open Wed. and Sun. 1.30–6.15 Apr. to Sept. Charge

Penshurst Place (4) Open daily (except Mon. and Fri.) 2–6 Easter to June, 1–6 July to Sept.

Leeds Castle (3) Open Tues., Wed., Thurs. and Sun. 1–5.30 Apr. to Sept. Charge

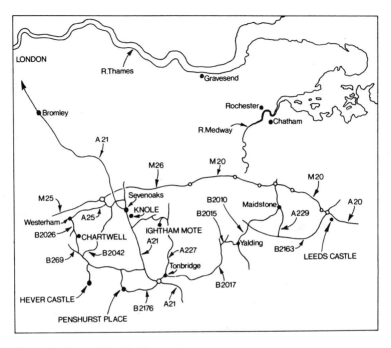

Tour 4 – Route (David Cheepen)

TOUR 5

London – Canterbury – Dover

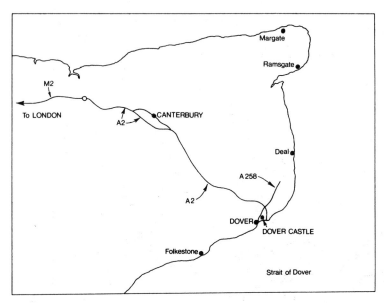

Tour 5 – Route (David Cheepen)

**Canterbury
   Cathedral (3)**

**West Gate (Canterbury)
   (3)**

**St. Augustine's   Open daily. Closed Sun. in winter till 2. Charge
   Abbey
(3) (Eng. Heritage)**

**St. Martin's
   Church (3)**

Greyfriars (3)   Open daily 1.30–5.30 Easter to Oct. Charge

Blackfriars (3)

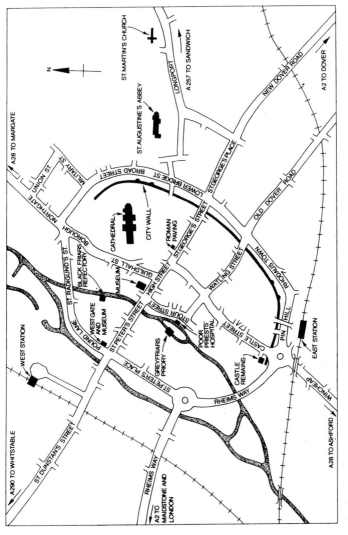

Canterbury – Sketch Map (David Cheepen)

Poor Priests'
Hospital (3)

Open weekdays 2–4 or 5. Also 10–1 in summer. Charge

Dover Castle (3)
(Eng. Heritage)

Open daily, Sun. from 2 (Sun. from 9.30, May to Sept.)

Roman lighthouse
(Pharos) (2)

(Enclosed by curtain walls of castle)

Roman Painted
House (2)

Open daily Apr. to Oct. Charge

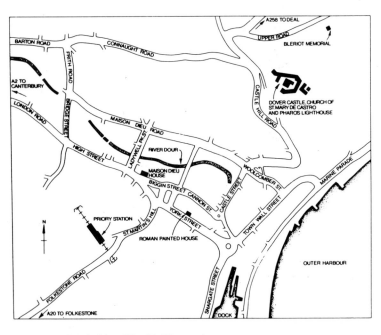

Dover – Sketch Map (David Cheepen)

TOUR 6

London – St. Albans – Hatfield House

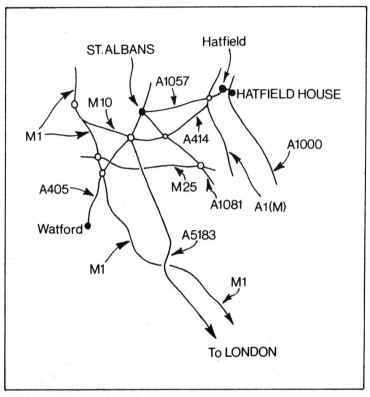

Tour 6 – Route (David Cheepen)

St. Albans
   Abbey (3)

Roman Museum (2) Open daily. Sun. from 2. Charge

Hypocaust (2)   (Museum controls access)

Theatre (2)   Open daily. Charge

Hatfield House (4) House and gardens open daily (except Mon.) Sun. from 2.30. Charge
Park: daily Apr. to Sept. Charge

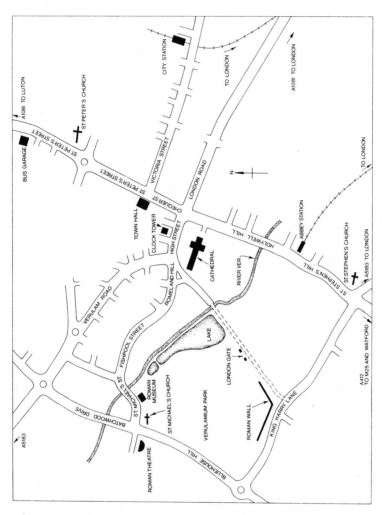

St. Albans – Sketch Map (David Cheepen)

Right: Tour 7 – Route (David Cheepen)

TOUR 7

(A) Coggeshall – Long Melford – Lavenham
London
(B) Ashwell – Wimpole Hall – Cambridge – Ely – Norwich – Blickling
Hall – Walsingham – Holkam Hall.

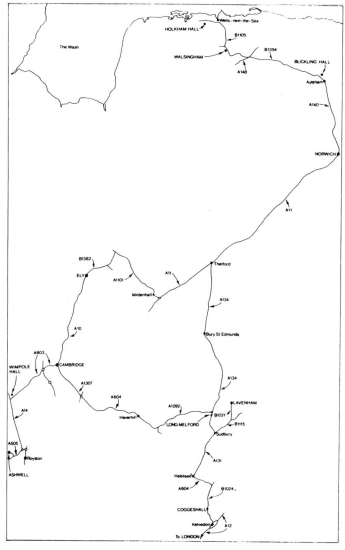

(A) Paycocke's House (Coggeshall) (3) (N.T.)

Open Tues., Thurs., Sun. 2–5.30 Apr. to Sept. Charge

Church – Coggeshall (3)

Church – Long Melford (3)

Melford Hall (4) (N.T.)

Open Wed., Thurs. and Sun. Also Sat. 2–6 (June, July and Aug.) Apr. to end Sept.

Kentwell Hall (4)

Open Wed. and Thurs. 2–6 Apr. to Sept. Also Sat. and Sun. 12–6 (July and Aug.) Charge

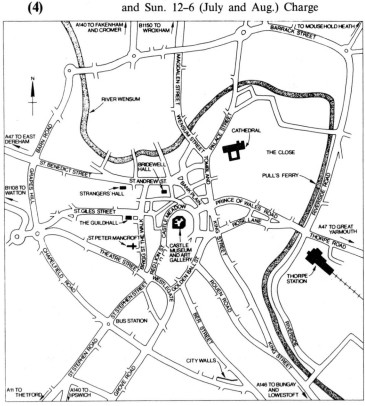

Norwich – Sketch Map (David Cheepen)

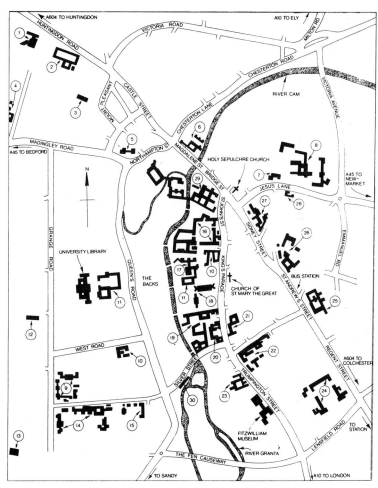

1 .Fitzwilliam College	11. Clare College	21. Corpus Christi College
2. New Hall College	12. Clare Hall	22. Pembroke College
3. St. Edmund's Hall	13. University College	23. Peterhouse College
4. Churchill College	14. Newnham College	24. Downing College
5. Westminster College	15. Ridley Hall	25. Emmanuel College
6. Magdalene College	16. Trinity College	26. Christ's College
7. Wesley College	17. Trinity Hall	27. Sidney Sussex College
8. Jesus College	18. King's College	28. Westcott House
9. Selwyn College	19. Queens' College	29. St. John's College
10. Gonville and Caius College	20. St. Catherine's College	30. Darwin College

Cambridge – Sketch Map (David Cheepen)

215

**Church –
Lavenham (3)**

**Guildhall –
Lavenham (3)
(N.T.)**   Open daily Apr. to Oct. Charge

**(B) Church –
Ashwell (3)**

**Wimpole Hall
(5)
(N.T.)**   Open daily (except Mon. and Fri. 1–5) April to Oct.

**Kings College
Cambridge (3)**

**St. Edward, King
and Martyr (4)**

Trinity College (4)

Ely Cathedral (3)

Norwich Cathedral (3)

**Strangers' Hall (3)
(Folk Museum)**   Open weekdays. Charge

**Blickling Hall (4)
(N.T.)**   Open daily (except Mon. and Thurs.) Apr. to Oct.

Walsingham (Shrine) (3)

Holkham Hall (5)   House open Sun., Mon. and Thurs. from 1.30 late-May to Sept. (Also Wed. July and Aug.) Charge Access to Park all year.

TOUR 8

London – Hardwick Hall – Haddon Hall – Cromford – Chatsworth – Eyam

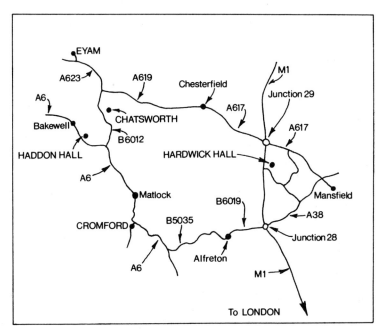

Tour 8 – Route (David Cheepen)

Hardwick Hall (4)
(N.T.)
Open Wed., Thurs., Sat. and Sun. 1–5.30 Easter to Oct.

Haddon Hall (3)
Open daily (except Sun. and Mon.) Apr. to Sept.

Arkwright's Cotton
Mill (5)

Chatsworth House
(4)
House open daily (except Mon. and Tues.) Sat. and Sun. from 1.30. Charge
Gardens: daily. Charge

Eyam (4)

TOUR 9

London – Bath – Wells – Glastonbury – Cadbury Castle – Exeter.

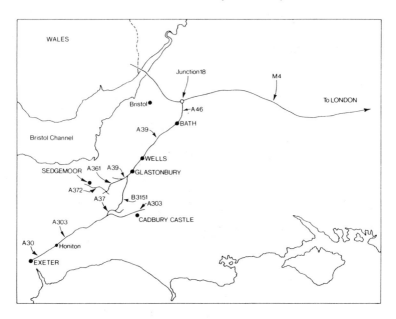

Tour 9 – Route (David Cheepen)

Bath Abbey (3)

Roman Baths (2)   Open daily (inclusive ticket for Baths, Pump Room and Assembly Rooms)

Grand Pump Room   Open daily. Sun. from 11 or 2
(5)

**Assembly
  Rooms (5)**   Open daily.

Wells Cathedral (3)

Glastonbury – Abbey ruins (3)   Open daily. Charge

Cadbury Castle (3)

Exeter Cathedral (3)

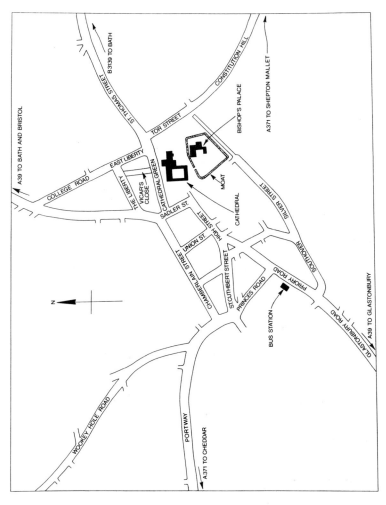

Wells – Sketch Map (David Cheepen)

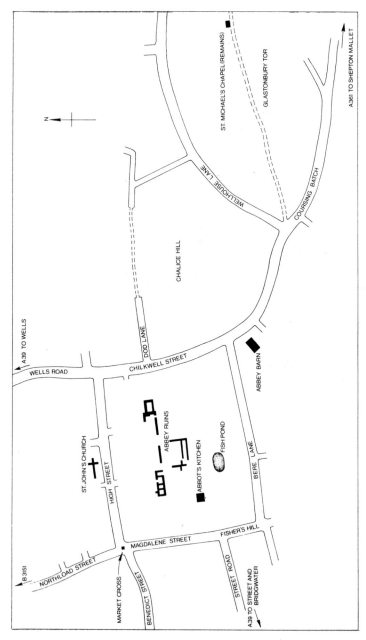

Glastonbury – Sketch Map (David Cheepen)

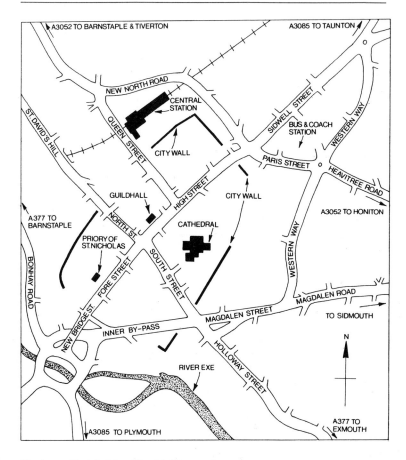

Exeter – Sketch Map (David Cheepen)

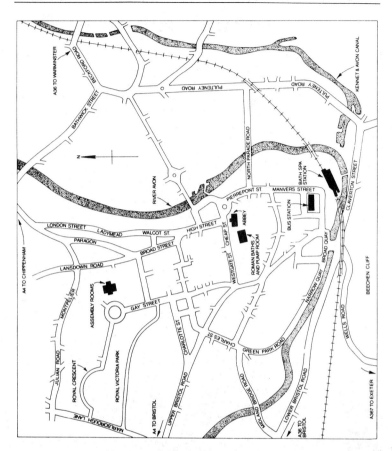

Bath – Sketch Map (David Cheepen)

TOUR 10

London – Winchester – Salisbury – Wilton House – Old Sarum – Stonehenge – Longleat

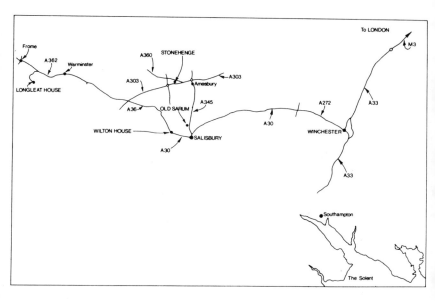

Tour 10 – Route (David Cheepen)

Winchester Cathedral (3)

Castle (Great Hall) (3) — Open weekdays. Sun. 2–4.30 (in summer). Charge

Salisbury Cathedral (3)

Mompesson House (5) (N.T.) — Open Sat. to Wed. Apr. to Oct. Also (by appointment) some weekends in Nov. and Dec. Charge

Wilton House (4) — Open daily (except Mon.). Sun. from 2. Apr. to Sept. Charge

Old Sarum (3) (Eng. Heritage) — Open daily (all Sun. in summer) Charge

Stonehenge (1) Open daily. Charge
(Eng. Heritage)

Longleat (4)   Open daily. Charge

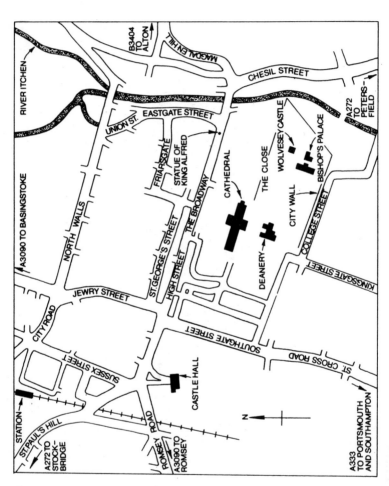

Winchester – Sketch Map (David Cheepen)

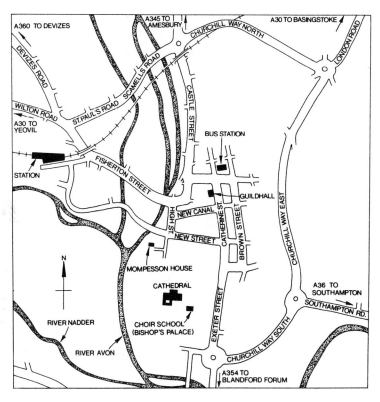

Salisbury – Sketch Map (David Cheepen)

TOUR 11

London – Dorchester – Maiden Castle – Higher Bockhampton – Tolpuddle
– Badbury Rings – Kingston Lacy – Corfe Castle

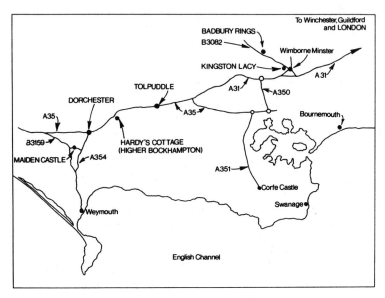

Tour 11 – Route (David Cheepen)

Dorchester

**Maiden Castle (1)
(Eng. Heritage)**

**Hardy's Cottage
(5) (N.T.)**   Open daily (except Tues. morning) April to Oct.

Tolpuddle (5)

Badbury Rings (2)

**Kingston Lacy (4)
(N.T.)**   House open Sat. to Wed. 1–5. Park: daily. Charge

Corfe Castle (3)   Open daily. Charge

226

TOUR 12

London – Stratford upon Avon – Ludlow – Stokesay Castle – Ironbridge –
Chester – Lake District (Grasmere)

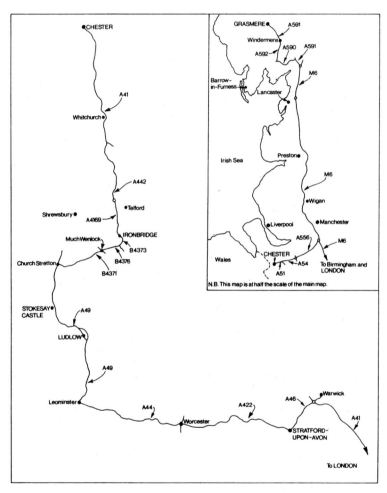

Tour 12 – Route (David Cheepen)

**Shakespeare's
Birthplace
(4)**

Open daily. (Sun. from 1.30 Nov. to March).
Charge (inclusive ticket available for all properties
of the Shakespeare Birthplace Trust)

227

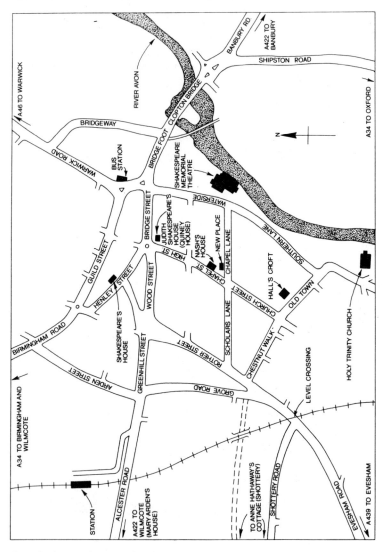

Stratford-upon-Avon – Sketch Map (David Cheepen)

Mary Arden's House (4)   Open daily (Sun 2–6 Apr. to Oct.) Not Sun. Nov. to March. Charge

Ann Hathaway's Cottage (4)   Open daily (not Sun. Nov. to March). Charge

Ludlow Castle (3)   Open daily. Sun. in winter on application. Charge

Stokesay Castle (3) (Eng. Heritage)   Open daily (except Tues.) Mar. to Oct. Nov. weekends only, and parties during the week by arrangement. Charge

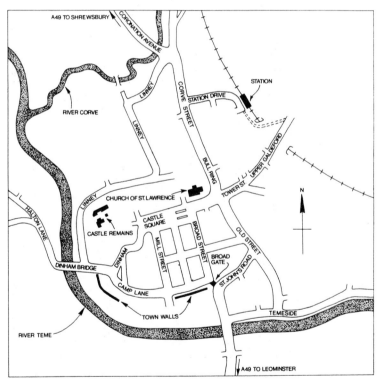

Ludlow – Sketch Map (David Cheepen)

Ironbridge Gorge Museum (5) Open weekdays. Charge (inclusive ticket obtainable at Visitors' Centre for 6 main sites)

Chester – Wall (2 and 3)
Cathedral (3)
Rows (3)

Grosvenor Museum (2) Open weekdays. Also Sun. in summer from 2.30

Dove Cottage (5) Open weekdays (closed mid-Jan. to Feb.) Charge

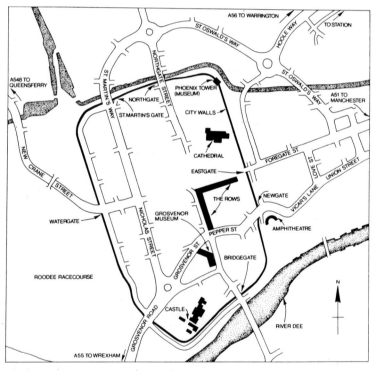

Chester – Sketch Map (David Cheepen)

TOUR 13

London – Burghley House (Stamford) – Lincoln

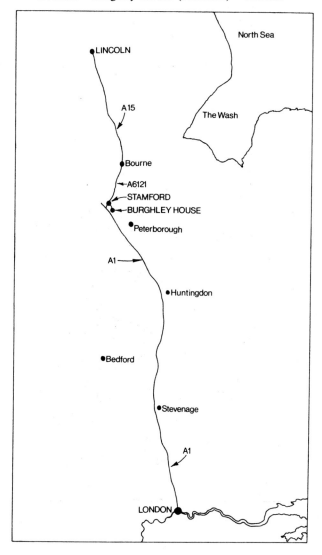

Tour 13 – Route (David Cheepen)

Burghley House (4) Open daily (except Mon. and Fri.). Sun. from 2.
Charge

Lincoln Cathedral (3)

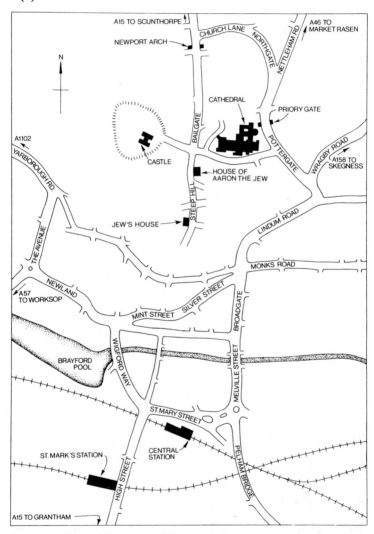

Lincoln – Sketch Map (David Cheepen)

TOUR 14

London – York – Fountains Abbey – Castle Howard

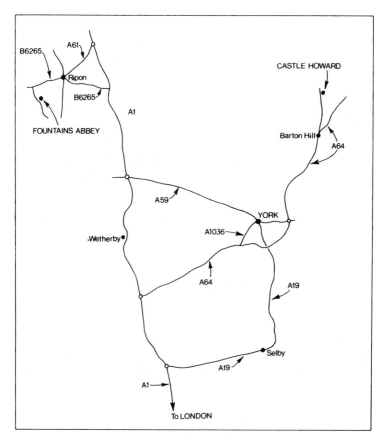

Tour 14 – Route (David Cheepen)

York Minster (3)

Wall (2 and 3)

Jorvik Viking Centre (3)   Open daily. Charge

Fountains Abbey (3) (N.T.) Open daily (charge includes Fountains Hall)

Castle Howard (4) Open daily (House from 1) Easter to Oct.

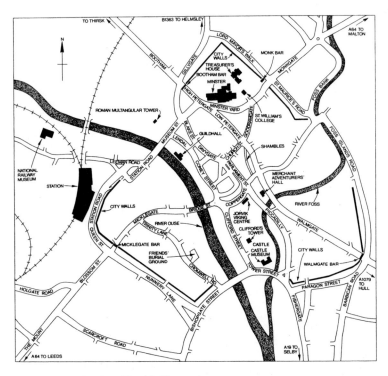

York – Sketch Map (David Cheepen)

TOUR 15

London – Durham – Jarrow – Hadrian's Wall – Warkworth – Alnwick – Dunstanburgh Castle – Bamburgh – Holy Island

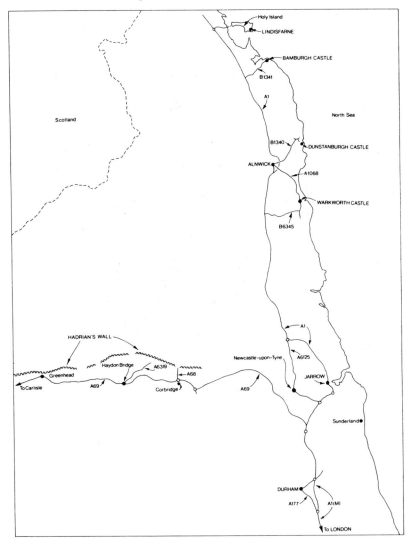

Tour 15 – Route (David Cheepen)

Durham Cathedral
  (3)

Jarrow (5)

Housesteads (2)   Open daily. Sun from 2. Oct. to Apr.
  (Eng. Heritage/N.T.)

Vindolanda (2)   Open daily. Charge
  (Eng. Heritage)

Warkworth Castle   Open daily. Sun. from 2. Oct. to Apr. Charge
  (3) (Eng.
  Heritage)

Alnwick Castle (3)   Open daily from 1 (except Fri. and Sat. May to
                          late-Sept.). Charge

Dunstanburgh   Open daily. Sun. from 2. Oct. to Apr. Charge
  Castle (3) (Eng.
  Heritage/N.T.)

Bamburgh Castle   Open daily from 2. Easter to Sept. Charge
  (3)

Holy Island –   Open daily. (All Sun. in Summer)
  Priory ruins (3)
  (Eng. Heritage)
  – Castle (3)   Open daily (except Fri.) Apr. to Sept. Charge
  (N.T.)

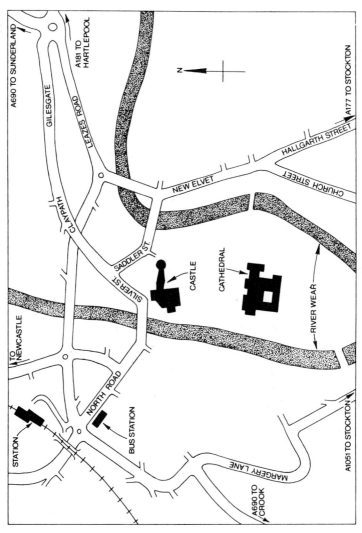

Durham – Sketch Map (David Cheepen)

Index

Notes